Professional Praise for this Commentary

"...masterful...meaningful to contemporary readers...raises important questions for reflection...useful spiritual advice...useful for learned readers, and scholarly specialists... excellent example of a contemporary attempt to make his classic work relevant for people of today who are looking for answers to the problems and meaning of life."
- Carl Olson, Professor of Religious Studies, Allegheny College

"Finally, a much-needed and sure to be cherished resource. If you've never read the Bhagavad Gita, this book is a perfect starting place. If you're a devotee of the Gita, this commentary will open new doors as you apply its teachings to our current struggles and realities...clear writing and compelling examples...shed tremendous new light on the universality and humanity of these teachings...essence of the Gita in examples which are compelling and real without compromising the power of the original. The story, so familiar to me, became completely new and completely familiar all at once. What a treasured resource this is sure to be."
- Claudia Horwitz, Author, Spiritual Activist

"There have been many translations and commentaries on Bhagavad Gita. Each one of them highlights a life that has been not only deeply touched but also inspired to touch others. (The author) is one of those touched souls.
...having absorbed this celestial song (he) brings us this translation... His style is different to that of many others. He has simplified a thousands of year old text and has restated its contents in today's non-sensical, logic driven, simple to use context. This translation of Bhagavad Gita is suited to such souls when they cry out for a meaning of life, its apparent joys and its apparent failings."
- Surinder Jain, Vice Chairman, Hindu Council of Australia

"Those of us who found other translations of the Bhagavad Gita more challenging will appreciate (Swamiji's) efforts. His translation allows us to gain insight into this great text and apply the knowledge to our everyday lives immediately!"
- Vicki Beilharz: Anusara Yoga Cert

T0099320

For His Holiness 1008 Sri Sri Srimat
Swami Narayan Tirthaji Maharaj [1915 - 2001]
who teaches me love of God, humanity, and nature.

Bhagavad Gita for Modern Times

Secrets to Attaining Inner Peace & Harmony

commentary by

Swami Sadashiva Tirtha

Sat Yuga Press
New York
http://satyuga.com

Bhagavad Gita for Modern Times
Secrets to Attaining Inner Peace & Harmony
Swami Sadashiva Tirtha
(author of *The Ayurveda Encyclopedia*)

© Copyright 2007 Swami Sadashiva Tirtha.
All rights reserved. First Edition: 3,000 copies

Illustrations © Copyright 2007 Jayanthi Noronha
All rights reserved.
No part of this book may be used or reproduced or transmitted in any way
without written consent from the publisher except or brief quotations used
in critical articles and reviews.

Softcover Edition:
ISBN-13: 978-0-9658042-6-4
ISBN-10: 0-9658042-6-7
Library of Congress Control
Number: 2007900258

PDF E-book Edition:
ISBN-13: 978-0-9658042-7-1
ISBN-10: 0-9658042-7-5

An audio-book edition is also available

Sanskrit Reviewer: Hari Prasad Bhatt Shastri, M.A. (Sanskrit).
Professor of Sanskrit, Mahavidhayalaya, Uttarkashi

Cover Design by Linda Parks:
The leaves of the sacred Peepal (Ashwatthama) tree.

Publisher: Sat Yuga Press
P.O. Box 94 Bayville, NY 11709 USA
http://satyuga.com

Sat Yuga Press is a member of
Green Press Initiative

Printed in Canada using vegetable inks, and 50% recycled covers (25% post consumer waste). Sat Yuga Press offsets all our carbon, tree, and water usage: for the love of earth ahimsa. See our 'socio-eco-positive' publisher policy online.

Table of Contents

Dedication

This book is for my students who, for the past decade, have been requesting I write a commentary on *Bhagavad Gita*; and for those who are looking to understand the wisdom of *Gita* as it directly applies to their daily lives;

This book is for all people seeking greater peace, harmony and balance of their spiritual priorities with their worldly goals and responsibilities.

This book is for all *bhaktas* (those of a devotional bent) who are seeking how to integrate *Vedanta* and *Bhakti* (balance intellectual and emotional spiritual development).

This book is for all those seeking some insight into the universality of religions, spirituality, nature, and ethics.

Acknowledgements

I'm grateful to a number of people who have helped bring this book into creation; the many students over the years suggesting I write this book, Ray Noronha who showed me an actual need to write it, Jayanthi Noronha for her inspiring drawings used at the end of each chapter, and Victor Simon who inspired me to actually seek its publication.

Also I am grateful to Guru Amrit Kaur Khalsa for her personal care in editing the manuscript; Hari Prasad Bhatt Shastri who ensured my translation of the Sanskrit *slokas* was accurate, Linda Parks who put her soul into designing the cover; and to Curt Matthews of IPG and his staff, Mark Noble, Mary Rowles, Erin McGee, Elisabeth Malzahn, and Jen Wisnowski, for their caring guidance while preparing this book.

Introduction

Why Another Commentary

For the past decade or so, many of my students have asked me to write a commentary on the *Bhagavad Gita*. Since great saints of the past like Adi Shankara have written superior commentaries, I saw no need. However in 2005, one of my students said, "I have not found any commentary on *Gita* that relates it's concepts to my religion. How does *karma* relate to Christianity, and how can I apply these insights in my daily life?' Moreover, he noted that many of his friends also have the same questions.

At first I was surprised, since it was my sense that simply by reading the *Gita*, one's contemplation would yield insights into how this wisdom relates to a modern life and religion. Still, since so many questions about the *Gita* remain unanswered, it suggested a need for this commentary.

Not fully convinced that it was necessary or even possible—couldn't imagine telling people how they should interpret the *Gita*—I agreed to write an introductory essay to help readers find a modern application for this ancient text. When I finished writing, I found that I had written a commentary for the entire Chapter 2. It seemed as though there was a book waiting to be written. So I cautiously tried another chapter. The writing flowed easily. It didn't take long before the entire commentary was complete.

Thereupon, I sent the work to people around the world, including the United States, Australia, and India, who had earlier requested a commentary to see if my musings answered their questions or clarified anything. The feedback was quite positive, and with some additional rewrites, the students felt they had the book they were looking for. I then set out to give seminars on the topic, here and abroad, for further live feedback. And I gave advanced copies to several *Gita* study groups for their reaction. People found the ideas useful and applicable to their own lives. Thus, it seemed the book addressed the issues of a wide international audience.

Still, as I feel one's best insights come from one's own private contemplation, this commentary is designed merely as a starting point and not as 'the way' to understand the *Gita*. It is a template, providing one way to integrate ancient universal ideas with today's issues. With this in mind, I humbly present a commentary of the *Bhagavad Gita* that may speak to the modern reader's life experiences. I pray to Veda Vyasa, the author of this text, that my work be true to the essence of his wisdom.

May you, dear readers, find some insight and solace from this book and may you grow ever more rapt in God-love. Namaskar, the God/highest spiritual state in me, honors the God/highest spiritual state in you.

Bayville, NY USA
February, 2007

Chapter 1
Realizing the Consequences of War

About The Gita - Overview

The *Bhagavad Gita* is considered the essence of the essence of India's esteemed Vedic philosophy. All the countless Vedic tomes written over the past 5,000 or so years are distilled into this short chapter of the great epic, the *Mahabharata*.

While Vedic literature comes from India and the Hindu religion, the teachings are really describing universal laws of nature (ie, universal codes of conduct and ways to live in tune with nature's harmony) and experiences common to people of all faiths. It was only conquering Britain that labeled the Indus valley people 'Indus' and called their culture the 'Indu religion' because they could not conceive of a culture that did not distinguish between life and spirit. The fact is, as in many ancient, indigenous cultures, there was no separate concept of 'religion,' because humans did not perceive themselves as separate from spirit; there is only sacred life.

A cursory review of cultures and religions will find many similarities at their essence. There is a saying in India, 'there are many paths, but one goal'. India was, and to some extent, still is a country that celebrates all paths to God. Even for those who don't believe in God, but believe in nature, or ethics, this too is accepted and celebrated. Anything positive is worshipped. Walk down a street in India and you will find walls with drawings of Krishna, Buddha, and Jesus. Such is the love and acceptance of the many paths leading to the one Supreme and Ultimate Goal.

This is not to suggest that all religions are the same: each has its own set of rituals, rites, and beliefs. But the essence of religions—one eternal God and God is love—is the same. *Bhagavad Gita* discusses the celebration of the Divine bliss of God as it applies to a personal relationship with God in each person's daily life. How does a sincere person balance worldly and Divine spheres? How can one be a helpful servant in the midst of obstacles and stresses? This is one of the great values of the teachings of the *Bhagavad Gita* that remains as relevant today as in ancient times.

Still, many people tell me they do not see much from this ancient story that can be applied to their lives, for example, 'Is this 5,000-year-old story relevant to modern-day life? Do the teachings apply to those who don't believe in God?' The answers to both questions are, yes. This book attempts to discuss the insights from the *Gita* as they apply to modern-day life, regardless of one's spiritual choices.

Ayurveda, a part of the Vedic literature, examines the universal principles of recovering and maintaining health and balance in life to grow on one's path to their spiritual goal. Ayurveda is founded on the universal spiritual principles of Vedic culture. Nowadays, people of all faiths find benefit in following their Ayurvedic lifestyle.

Daily we are helped by people of different faiths—doctors, dentists, teachers, police, soldiers, cooks, neighbors—we don't feel uneasy or threatened by their spiritual beliefs. So, too, reading the insights of the *Bhagavad Gita* should be just as natural. Moreover, Hinduism is not an evangelistic religion—it does not seek to convert others.

When I was a child, there was a company called Levy's selling Jewish rye bread. Their slogan was, You don't have to be Jewish to love Levy's. So, too, you don't have to be Hindu to learn from the *Gita*.

Yoga

This term is used as the foundation or interwoven fabric of this current interpretation, so it is important to define the term. *Yoga* has several meanings, but ultimately it means to unite, harmonize, or to make into one.

In recent years, many people have understood *yoga* to mean stretching postures—commercials show people in *yoga* positions. This form of *yoga* (*asanas* or postures) helps strengthen and flex the body, and enhances mind-body harmony. In turn, this reduces physical and emotional stress and prepares one for deeper spiritual progress in meditation. What happens through the *asanas* (poses) is that the different energies in the body become harmonized or united—all funneling, or dovetailing into one readily accessible channel for energy, clarity, and positivity.

Yoga means union. In the case of poses, it unites the mind and body and the energies. The deepest level of *yoga* (or union) means realizing one's inner eternal Soul unites with the universal Soul (Self-Realization). In reality, since the Soul is eternal, it is already united; however, it takes an inner awakening to realize this union or *yoga*. According to Vedic philosophy, the goal of life is to awaken (harmonize or unite) one's inner awareness (or consciousness) and that its true nature is eternal Soul or God or nature or ethics—or whatever personal belief system you subscribe to.

We are not limited. Believing that we *are* limited is what causes suffering. If a person sees something that they desire (eg, a breathtaking sunset, a double chocolate fudge brownie, a puppy, a Porsche), they are saying, 'I don't have that and I want it so I that will feel happier'. The Vedic view is that not only do you already have it, but it is a part of who you are—it is the same eternal Soul. But when a person is not aware of this, they feel a separation from external objects, and this separation causes longing that leads to suffering. Desires denied result in frustration, anger, depression, greed, and theft.

Yet, even when a person gets what they want (a puppy, the Porsche), it does not bring complete and eternal happiness. This creates more confusion and frustration, and a vicious cycle develops. Eventually, when people cannot feel lasting satisfaction, they develop unhealthy philosophical outlooks on life (eg, I don't deserve to be happy, that is why I never can find lasting happiness; God is vindictive, always teasing me, but never giving me such peace. I'll have to find happiness in gaining all the fame and fortune possible.)

All of this misses the essential point that by going within, one finds a reservoir of Divine peace, nectar, and lasting contentment that is more compelling than anything that the outer world can give. By uniting one's inner personal Soul with the eternal Soul, life gradually changes from confusion, struggle and strife, to graceful, childlike wonder, harmony, and self-referential joy.

So *yoga*, in its highest context, can be said to be a path or method to Self-Realization or Self-Unification. While this is indeed a lofty ideal, the *Bhagavad Gita* explains how, through simple daily life experiences, people can culture this union within themselves, their families, and communities.

Still, by defining the term *yoga* with other large concepts such as Self-Realization, the result can be further confusion, leaving many people unsure and unable to grasp the idea. So the message of the *Bhagavad Gita* is simply that the aim of life is to live in ever greater peace and harmony through ever intimate connection with God. God is love, the word is love. This is Krishna's message in the *Gita*.

Lord Krishna, the teacher in the *Gita*, is a representative form of God (like Jesus). God is eternal and unmanifest; Krishna, therefore, can only represent an aspect of God Almighty. Hindu's consider Krishna an *avatar*, that is, God taking a human form. Like Jesus, Krishna's message is a simple message of love. Jesus too, came from God and took human form on this earth. There are many parallels between them when we get past the semantics.

Krishna is a Divine parent, only wanting to see His children happy. So, in *Gita*, Krishna is telling them how to be truly happy. Mundane life (material objects like cars, money, and fame) brings temporary happiness. To be truly happy, find that which never stops giving bliss—uniting or hugging God, holding God's hand each and every day in life, each and every moment of the day. This is the message.

While Hindus believe in the one eternal God, they also acknowledge that God takes human form to become more reachable. It is very difficult to ask someone to imagine that which cannot be imagined, that is, something without form, beyond thought or feeling. So, God, in compassion, takes a form from time to time to give people a more easily grasped model or a metaphor to follow. It is easier to have a loving relationship with someone who is near than with someone whom you don't see for decades because they live on the other side of the globe. In the same way, God makes the extra effort, knowing that it is quite difficult for humans to follow an impersonal Being.

Yoga or Self-Realization is then simply a union, a loving embrace between a person and God. Remembering God, remembering the eternal spirit keeps one's spirit ever rising higher in the long-term view. How to live an endearing, precious, grateful, sacred life with God and avoid the pitfalls that can separate you from God are the teachings of this book.

The ideas stated here are universal, because they do not specifically refer to any personal rituals found in any one religion. These ideas evoke different insights for different people, whatever path they follow. All that the reader need remember is that the *Bhagavad Gita* is a loving how-to book to help you learn how to see yourself with the highest possible self-worth—that is, as a loving spirit—and how to share that loving spirit with other spirits, including all of God's children, creatures, and nature, and with God.

Universal Parallels

Many people requested that this commentary include parallels to other religions. To the degree that the author has some knowledge of other religions, such insights have been incorporated. The reader will get the most out of this book by noting the parallels from their own spiritual paths. You are welcome to send these insights to the author for inclusion in future editions of this book.

There is the story of the blind people and the elephant. Each describes an elephant by what they experience. Feeling the leg, one says an elephant is pillar-like. Another feeling the ear says elephant is flat and thin. Still a third feels the belly and says elephant is big and round. Yet another feels the trunk and says the elephant is thin and cylindrical. All are describing one aspect of elephant, but none can see the whole elephant. In the same way, each person describes God from his or her limited human experience. But like the elephant, God is much greater and goes beyond description. The Vedic view of spiritual life is 'live and let live'. It is sufficient that one experiences something spiritual in life; the 'what' and the 'how' is insignificant.

The Events Leading to the Story

To bring you up to speed on what is happening in the story when we enter the picture (or as they say on TV, previously in the Life of Arjuna), here is a synopsis of the events leading up to the *Bhagavad Gita*.

The story of the *Mahabharata* (the Great Bharat) is based on the wisdom of the respected King Bharat, whose great contribution to ancient India was to break up the dogma of the caste system by saying that it is not the caste you are born into that makes you great, rather, it is your own efforts and actions in your life that earn you such recognition. King Bharat established a form of democracy, where everyone had an equal right to succeed and flourish in the world from their own efforts. Caste is discussed in detail in chapter 4 (verse 13) and chapter 18 (verse 41–45).

For some ages before this, if a person was born into a class (eg, the priest class), they were automatically respected and obeyed—even if they were incompetent or dishonest. People were not seen as equals. It was through the wisdom and courage of King Bharat that such a misinterpretation of Vedic culture was dispelled. In gratification of his efforts, the people voted to name their country, Bharat. This is the real name of India. (It was only the British who called the people of Bharat [Bharatas], the people living in the Indus valley, Indians and called their country India.)

Moving ahead in time, a succeeding King of Bharat was yet another great king, looking out for the welfare of the people before his own needs. He had several sons and they were called the Pandava family. The King had a brother who had one son, Duryodhana; they were called the Kurus family. While the king's sons were growing up wise, and strong, courageous and adored by all, the king's nephew, Duryodhana, was of poor character, dishonest, and jealous of his cousins. To make matters worse, the uncle spoiled his son, giving him everything he wanted and never raising him with discipline.

Because obtaining material possessions cannot make a person truly satisfied, Duryodhana became empty and bitter; he had never learned that to be truly rich you must give your love away and work for the welfare of others.

As fate would have it, the good king was forced to bequeath his kingdom to his brother. This was seen as a great opportunity for Duryodhana to steal the kingdom from his good cousins, the Pandavas. The Pandava brothers were five in number, Arjuna, the archer, is the main character in the *Bhagavad Gita.*

Through Duryodhana's treachery, he managed to steal the kingdom from the Pandavas. His father, the newly installed king Dhritaraashtra, continued to spoil his son, siding with all he did and never reprimanding him for his dishonest ways. Yet, even with stealing the kingdom from the Pandavas, Duryodhana's greed and jealousy could not be eased, as is the nature of an empty inner life. Only one thought pervaded Duryodhana's mind, kill the Pandavas. After many failed nefarious attempts, he decided to challenge them to war. Knowing that the King and all his great sage warriors and counselors would be forced to take his side as they swore an oath to the King, Duryodhana pushed for war.

All the elders tried to dissuade him from this unspeakable idea. Even Lord Krishna, cousin to both the Pandavas and Kurus, could not change his mind. It is for this reason that Lord Krishna (an avatar, or God taking human birth to uphold the righteous whenever unrighteousness is poised to gain the upper hand in society) took birth at this time to restore the balance of goodness in the world.

When all options to dissuade Duryodhana from war failed, Lord Krishna finally sat with Arjuna (the good cousin) and Duryodhana (the jealous cousin) and made the following offer: he said that since he was God, it was unfair for him to fight on either side because that would guarantee his side would win. So one cousin could choose Krishna's armies, weapons, and vehicles, while and the other cousin could choose Krishna to be his chariot driver and guide.

The materialistic-minded Duryodhana, seeing only worldly things as power sources, chose the armies, weapons, and vehicles. Arjuna said, 'I don't want anything other than to be on God's side.' And so it was, both cousins got what they wanted. The battle is now set and so begins the teaching of the *Bhagavad Gita* just before the great battle.

When read on the purely mundane level, some people use the *Gita* as an excuse for war, citing Lord Krishna admonishing Arjuna to fight. But understanding the causes leading up to the war, one realizes nothing could be further from the truth. Duryodhana had one mission on his mind, ethnic cleansing of the Pandava race. All the sages, and Krishna himself unsuccessfully tried to change his mind. So Krishna told Arjuna he needs to prevent his race from being eradicated. There is no approval here of fighting, simply because you disagree with another's views, or because other people are making your life difficult. In *Gita*, war is accepted only as a last-resort protection from annihilation.

Moreover, for those who only read *Gita* for its worldly accounts miss the timeless secrets to finding true, lasting inner peace, devotion, and harmony that are the only foundation to world peace. One message in *Gita* states if you apply it's teachings to your personal, spiritual, and family life, automatically, such applications will bring peace and harmony into the world at large. To the saying, 'wars are fought in the mind's of men', *Gita* answers, cultivate peace in the minds and there will be no wars.

The battle in *Gita* can be then viewed as a metaphor for life-battles, where, from time to time people need to face challenges, confront ideas and stand up for who they are and what they believe in.

The focus of this commentary, then, is twofold,

- This is a guidebook applicable for modern times, revealing universal secrets so that anyone may achieve peace and harmony, follow their compassion, values, and visions to make the word a better place; and to develop a palpable devotion to God, God's children, and to nature, even in the midst of life-responsibilities and hectic outer events.

- The war and Arjuna's conflict about fighting is a metaphor. People can learn how to deal with stressful situations that require a person to speak up when they see injustice, inequality, and a lack of fairness—be it a family squabble. a work- or communi-ty-related issue, or a national policy; always remembering point one, that inner peace is the prerequisite for true and lasting un-derstanding and harmony in the outer realm. History is replete with failed movements that killed in the name of peace and in the name of God. If you want peace, be peace. If you want a lov-ing world, discover greater divine love within. As Gandhi said, 'be the change you wish to see.'

We have now discussed the history of the *Gita* and the events pre-cipitating the war. On the following page the actual story of the *Bhagavad Gita* begins.

The Gita Begins

As the battle was about to begin, on the field known as Kurukshtera, the Kurus were on one side, and the Pandavas were on the other side. Each had their armies and their supporting armies from other nations. In order to asses the situation, Arjuna requested that Krishna bring his chariot to the middle of the battlefield to view his enemies. [Verse 1–25]

Dhritarashtra said:
O Sanjaya, tell me what happened on the battlefield at Kurukshetra between my people and the Pandavas? [1]

Sanjaya answered:
Your son, Prince Duryodhana, observing the Pandava sons' armies, spoke to his teacher, Drona, and said [2]

See the mighty army of the sons of Pandava, arrayed by the son of Drupada, thy sagacious student. [3]

Here are the brave bowmen, who are equally adept warriors as Bhima and Arjuna in battle — the great soldiers, Yuyudhana, Virata, Drupada the charioteer. [4]

Valorous Drishtaketu Chekitana, fearless Kashiraja, Purujit, Kunti-Bhoja, and Shaibya - a man among men. [5]

There is dauntless Yudhamanyu, valiant Uttamaujas, Subhadhra's son, and the sons of Draupadi — each of them mighty car-warriors. [6]

Now acquaint yourself with the distinguished warriors on our side. Here are the names of our army's captains: [7]

Here we have thyself, Bhishma, Karna, and Kripa, victors of battle, Ashvatthaman, Vikarna, Somadatta's son Bhurisrava, and Jayadratha. [8]

We have many other heroes skilled in battle and armed with diverse weaponry, vowed to lay down their lives for my sake. [9]

Our army, commanded by Bhishma is inadequate, whereas their army led by Bhima is up for the task. [10]

Therefore, let us keep all our army at their stations, protecting Bhishma. [11]

Then Bhishma, the valiant grandshire of the Kuru dynasty, roared like a lion and then loudly blew his conch shell to inspire Duryodhana. [12]

Then other conches blew, and kettledrums, tabors, trumpets and cow-horns resounded. It was a tremendous noise. [13]

Then Madhava (Krishna) and Pandava (Arjuna), who were in their chariot, yoked to white horses, also blew their divine conchs. [14]

Hrishikesha (Krishna) blew his conch shell (named) Panchajanya, Dhananjaya (Arjuna) blew his conch shell (named) Devadatta, and Vrikodara (Bhima), one of great prowess, blew his conch shell (named) Paundra. [15]

King Yudhishthira, son of Kunti blew his conch shell named Anantavijaya. Nakula, and Sahadeva blew their conch shells respectively named Sughosa and Manipushpaka. [16]

The great bowman, Kashiraja, and the mighty warrior Shikhandi, Dhrishtadyumna, Virata, and the unconquered hero, Satyaki; [17]

Drupada, sons of Draupadi, the mighty-armed son of Subhadra, all blew their own conchs, O King. [18]

This tremendous uproar vibrated into the sky and earth, shattering the hearts of Dhritarashtra's sons. [19]

Then O King, seeing Dhritharashtra's army now ready for battle, Arjuna, whose ensign was the monkey (Hanuman), raised his bow and spoke to Krishna. [20]

Arjuna said:
O Krishna, please drive this chariot between the armies so I might observe my enemies arrayed for battle, with whom I have to fight. [21 – 23]

Sanjaya said:
O King, Krishna complied and steered the chariot between the two armies. [24]

They stood in front of Bhishma, Drona, and all the rulers of the earth. Krishna said, behold Arjuna, all the assembled members of the Kuru dynasty are gathered here. [25]

Upon viewing the enemy, he saw his dearest teachers, cousins, and gurus who had lovingly raised and taught the Pandavas from childhood, and who now, because of their loyalty oaths to the king, were forced to take the side of the unjust Duryodhana and his father, King Dhritaraashtra. He also saw some of his friends, and some of his own sons, and his grandsons, who too were obliged to protect the King and so were on the side of the enemy. [Verse 26]

> *Arjuna saw both armies contained his relatives; grandfathers, fathers-in-law, uncles, brothers, cousins, his own sons, and grandsons, comrades, friends, and teachers. [26]*

Seeing these dear ones, who make up his life, Arjuna had a shocking realization. His feelings, his compassion for these beloved brethren stole his focus for war.

Arjuna said,
O Krishna, my mind was set on destroying the enemy, but now as I look at who comprises them, I see all the people who I grew up with, who loved me and raised me, and taught me to be a warrior. I see my childhood friends, and I see some of my own sons and grandsons. Suddenly my body shivers, the hairs on my skin stand on end, and my bow (and arrow) slip from my hands. My mouth is dry, my mind is spinning, and I am confused. I see bad omens.

What use is killing these beloved people? I wish neither victory nor kingdom. What is the value of life if killing them be the cost? What happiness would be derived from killing our own family? Would this not be sin brought upon our own selves? I'd rather let them kill me than live on after killing them.

So saying, Arjuna, having an anxiety attack, slunk down to the seat of the chariot. [Verse 27–47]

> *Realizing for the first time that he would be fighting his many beloved relatives, Arjuna, son of Kunti, became overwhelmed with compassion, and spoke in a grief-stricken manner. [27]*
>
> *Arjuna said:*
> *O Krishna, seeing my kinsmen gathered and ready for battle, my limbs are shaking and my mouth is dry. [28]*
>
> *My body shivers and the hairs are standing on end. My bow (Gandiva) slips from my hand. My skin is burning. [29]*
>
> *O Keshava (Krishna), I cannot stand properly, my mind is spinning, and I see inauspicious omens. [30]*
>
> *I see no good in killing my kinsmen. I don't care for any victory, or kingdom, or pleasures. [31]*

My teachers, uncles, sons, grandsons, grandfathers, fathers-in-law, brothers-in-law, and other kinsmen, only for the goal of attaining empire, pleasure, and enjoyment, they are willing to kill or be killed. Of what value is a kingdom, enjoyment, or even life O Govinda (Krishna)? [32 – 34]

I have no wish to kill, and would rather be killed than to end the lives of my kinsmen. I don't even care to rule the three worlds, let alone this earth. [35]

O Krishna, what pleasure is to be gained by killing these relatives? We would incur sin by killing these evil ones. [36]

So I suggest we not kill the sons of Dhritarashtra (our relations) because, how can we find any happiness by killing our family? [37]

While these enemies are overcome with greed, they don't see the evil, sinful results from killing their family members. [38]

So why shouldn't we just turn away from the sin as wee see clearly the evil in destroying the family? [39]

With the destruction of the family, their spiritual traditions also perish. When spirituality is destroyed, the family becomes unrighteous. [40]

O Krishna, when unrighteousness prevails, the women in the family become corrupt; and from corrupted women, undesirable progeny are born. [41]

The heinous deeds of those who destroy the family, give rise to an undesirable generation who do not follow family and community traditions, and thus the ancestors also fall as there is no offering made to them. [42]

From these nefarious deeds, new generations of undesirable people pervade the earth, destroying all spiritual traditions, and all noble lineages. [43]

O Krishna, I have heard that people, whose family spiritual traditions are destroyed, become residents of hell. [44]

Alas, we are ready to commit great sin because of greedy desire for kingdom, wealth and pleasure. [45]

It would be better for me if the sons of Dhritarashtra, with weapons in hand, slay me on the battlefield, unresisting and unarmed. [46]

Sanjaya said:
Airing his thoughts to Krishna, Arjuna sank down on the chariot seat, casting aside his bow and arrows; his mind overwhelmed in deep sorrow. [47]

Modern-Day Discussion Exercises

Who has not had some confrontation, some choice to make, to stand up for what they feel is right, even when it means going against loved ones—family, friends, or bosses and co-workers? Here are just a few examples of the same situation that occurs in modern life.

- What do you do when you learn your company or boss is cheating the employees, the country, harming the earth or the citizens?

- What does a student do when their friend tells them about some mischievous plans they have to deface their school, or worse, to harm students at school?

- What do you do when a beloved relative, friend, or teacher suddenly chooses a course you feel is unethical?

- What do you do when your friends tease or hurt someone just because they are different from you emotionally, culturally, or with regard to race or religion?

- What do you do when family or friends asks you to behave according to what is politically correct or culturally acceptable, yet you feel you are not being yourself?

Do you stand up against the status quo or peer pressure and speak what you feel is right, or do what you feel is right—whatever the consequence; even at the expense of being ostracized or worse?

As a result of seeing the human side of his 'enemy,' Arjuna had an anxiety attack. Unable to decide what to do, he became numb. So with the basic premise laid out, the underlying spiritual or ethical question becomes,

- How do you choose what is real?

- How do you determine what is important?

- Do ethics supersede relationships with loved ones?

- Do ethics prevail over peer pressure?

- Is war ever worth fighting when standing up for what you feel is righteous, gets others killed, hurt, or punished?

- Is there sin attached to your actions during war?

Life doesn't seem to be black and white, but rather many shades of gray.

These are basic questions that people today are forced ask themselves from time to time. With these basic questions in Arjuna's mind, the groundwork is set for Lord Krishna's reply. From Chapter 2 on, comes the teaching of Lord Krishna to Arjuna.

Krishna guides Arjuna's chariot into battle

Chapter 2
How to Attain Peace
Through Spiritual Understanding

The *Bhagavad Gita* is the essence—the cream of the crop—of Vedic philosophy. Here, in Chapter 2, is the essence of the *Gita*.

How does Krishna answer Arjuna's questions? How does Krishna deal with Arjuna's anxiety attack? How does God answer our prayers? How does life unfold for us when we become confused, anxious, nervous, worried, angry, or impatient? Or when the rug is pulled out from under us, and we are at our lowest point, or when we are falling. How does life unfold?

In this situation, Lord Krishna treats Arjuna with great respect and strength; he talks to his courage and wisdom.

Krishna says,
O Arjuna, how is it that depression comes to you at this moment of decision and action? You are, and have always shown yourself to be clear-minded, knowing your priorities, and strong in heart. Why suddenly now do you show such uncharacteristic behavior? [Verse 1–3]

Sanjaya said:
Lord Krishna spoke to the grief-stricken Arjuna, whose teary eyes were overwhelmed by compassion. [1]

Lord Krishna said:
O Arjuna, from where does this anxiety and depression arise, at this critical juncture? It is unfitting honorable people, and prevents entering heaven. [2]

O Arjuna do not yield to unmanliness, it is not worthy of you. O terror of enemies, cast off this faint-heartedness and rise up. [3]

Repeating his concerns, Arjuna now states that he will not fight—he chooses to be a conscientious objector. [Verse 4–10]

Arjuna said
O Krishna, destroyer of enemies, how can I point my arrows in battle against Bhishma and Drona who are are worthy of worship? [4]

Rather than kill these great Souls, it is better to live in this world as a beggar; otherwise, by killing them, all the spoils of war we attain will be stained with blood. [5]

It is not clear to me which is better, for us conquer them or for us to be conquered by them. If we kill the sons of Dhritarashtra, we would lose the will to live. [6]

My nature is overwhelmed with pity and depression, my mind confused about my true duty. I beg you Krishna, clearly instruct me on what is good for me, I am your disciple, and have taken refuge in you. [7]

Even if I win dominion over the earth and prosper, I don't know what can remove my sense-withering grief. [8]

Sanjaya said:
Having stated his quandary, Arjuna, conqueror of enemies, said: "I shall not fight, O Govinda." And fell silent. [9]

O Dhritarashtra, in the midst of the two armies, Krishna, as if smiling, spoke these words to the grief-stricken Arjuna. [10]

What is Real Does Not Change

Now Krishna begins his explanation, starting from the most spiritual insights, moving to the more mundane reasons for Arjuna to fight.

Krishna says,
You are upset for having to kill these people. Although what you say seems wise, it is not: you know no one dies. People are Souls, not bodies. Souls are eternal, bodies only house the Soul. The truly wise mourn neither for the dead nor the living.

All of us Souls have lived before in other bodies. Just as the Soul remains in the body as it changes from childhood to old age. So, too, the Soul remains as we change from one body to another. [Verse 11–13]

Lord Krishna said:
You are mourning for those who deserve not sorrow, yet you speak apparently as a wise person. The truly learned neither laments for the dead or the living. [11]

There never was a time I did not exist, nor you, nor all these kings. Nor is there ever a time that any of us shall cease to exist. [12]

Just as the Soul passes through this body from childhood to youth and old age, so too the Soul reincarnates from one body to another. Thus the wise never become confused by the true nature of the Soul. [13]

Remember that we experience physical sensations such as heat and cold, pleasure and pain, through our senses. They are temporal, because they have a beginning and an ending. These experiences will eventually pass. If the mind is focused solely on ever-changing sensory experiences, it will not be possible to quiet the mental chatter long enough to realize one's eternal Soul.

That which is real is nonchanging (eternal); that which is unreal is nonpermanent. So the ever-changing world can be said to be nonexistent, because it is not permanent. Only the Soul can be said to exist, because it is the one thing that does not change.

Knowing that the Souls of those you love are eternal and cannot ever die, fight this injustice. [Verse 14–18]

O son of Kunti, it is only due to the interaction of the senses and sense objects that cause feelings of heat, cold, pleasure, and pain. They are temporary experiences, with a beginning and an end. Therefore try to endure them. [14]

O men among men, wise people are serene and not imbalanced by these sensations, remaining equipoised in pleasure and pain. This is the only way to be ready for liberation. [15]

The unreal world has no existence and the real world can never end. The knowers of truth see this reality. [16]

Know that what pervades all matter is eternal; this Soul cannot be destroyed. [17]

The body perishes, but the Soul in bodies is eternal, indestructible, and infinite. So fight O Arjuna. [18]

The Soul is eternal; it always existed, and always will exist. It doesn't move, create, or change anything. So if a person is really the Soul, how can the Soul-Person be a killer if the Soul doesn't do anything other than exist?

When clothes wear out, we don't grieve too much about it; we simply buy new clothes. So too, the body is a covering for the Soul to wear in order for Self-Realization to have a form to realize its true eternal Soul. So when the body becomes old and unable to be a sturdy home for the Soul, the Soul casts off the old worn-out body and takes on a new one to continue the path to realize one's true eternal nature (Self-Realization). [Verse 19–25]

One who believes the Soul is a killer, or thinks that the Soul is killed knows not the Truth; Soul neither slays or is slain. [19]

The Soul is never born, nor ever dies. The Soul is unborn, eternal, changeless, timeless; it is not destroyed when the body is destroyed. [20]

O Arjuna, how can one kill anyone, when they know the Soul as eternal, unborn, and indestructible. [21]

Just as a person throws out old clothes and wears a new attire, like that, the Soul lets go of old, worn out bodies and takes on new bodies. [22]

Weapons cannot harm the Soul, fire cannot burn it, water cannot wet it, and air cannot dry it. [23]

The Soul cannot be pierced, burned, wet, or dried. It is eternal, omnipresent, unmoving, unchanging, and everlasting. [24]

The Soul is unmanifest, unknowable, immutable; therefore knowing this to be true, there is no reason to grieve. [25]

Now, if this talk of Soul is too abstract, Krishna next speaks from the mundane vantage; even from this view, there is no cause for grieving. From the point of view of life and death, we know that everything is born, lives, and eventually dies. So why grieve over the inevitable? [Verse 26–30]

O mighty-armed, even if you think the Soul continually revolves in the rebirth/death cycle, even then, there is no reason to grieve. [26]

Everything that is born, must die. And everything that dies, is born again. Therefore there is no cause to lament over inevitabilities. [27]

O Arjuna, we know nothing before and after birth; we only know things during life. So why grieve over the unknowable? [28]

Some see the Soul as wondrous, others speak of its wonder; some hear of the amazing Soul, and some, even after hearing about it still do not comprehend it. [29]

The Soul within the body of every living being is immortal; therefore, O Arjuna, you needn't grieve over any creature. [30]

If you should be killed in battle, defending the helpless or the righteous, if you are killed doing your life-purpose, your God-given duties, then you shall go to heaven. If you are victorious, you shall enjoy heaven on earth. So for all these reasons, son of your mother (Kunti), resolve your mind and heart and fight the good fight.

Knowing the true permanent nature of the Soul and the ever-changing and impermanent nature of life, see no difference between pleasure and pain, and winning and losing. Focus on the eternal, focus on inevitability, focus on duty, and you cannot incur sin. Sin is a function of the ever-changing world. It occurs when you focus on or get stuck in the relative world: this is sin. Acting beyond change, acting for eternity, takes you beyond sin. This is known as Self-Realization (*Moksha*) [Verse 31–38]

Considering your life-purpose (dharma) is upholding righteousness, you should not waver; there is nothing more purposeful than fulfilling your life purpose. [31]

O Arjuna, fortunate are those who are forced to uphold righteousness in an unsought war; it is a open gateway to heaven for such a soldier. [32]

Conversely, if you do not fight in this righteous war, you abandon your spiritual duty and reputation, and thus incur sin. [33]

People will speak ill of you; for honorable and esteemed people, dishonor is worse than death. [34]

> *These great chariot warriors will interpret your inaction as fear, and for those who once had high regard for you, you will be seen in disgrace. [35]*
>
> *Your enemies will maliciously insult you and discredit your heroism. What can be more painful than this? [36]*
>
> *If you are killed in battle you will attain heaven; if you are victorious in this war you will enjoy the earth. Therefore, O Arjuna, with a resolved mind, arise and fight. [37]*
>
> *Be equal minded in pleasure and pain, win and loss, victory and defeat; fight this battle. In this way, no sin will be attached to you. [38]*

Now the spiritual kernel of Vedic philosophy is presented: Self-Realization and the mechanics of how bondage is caused and how one can remove the bonds to realize their true nature, the eternal Soul.

Krishna says,

Let us now talk about *yoga*—the action that merges the inner self with the universal Self, the realization of this eternal nature of Self. If you are sincere, even a small amount of time devoted to *yoga* delivers you from fear. For this wisdom will free you from the bondage of actions of cause and effect (*karma*). Focus on your goals, or on the things that must be done without distraction. [Verse 39–41]

> *So I have explained to you the wisdom of Self-Realization. Now, listen about yoga of action without desire for reward; the knowledge of which frees one from the karmic bonds of cause and effect. [39]*
>
> *In this yoga there is no wasted effort or negative consequences. Even a little, sincere practice of yoga saves one from great fear. [40]*
>
> *O Arjuna, in this yoga, the sincere, resolved mind is focused and one-pointed; but the mind full of desires is scattered in many directions like branches on a tree. [41]*

Avoid people's words (spoken or written) just because they sound nice—that is, if they are the words of a charismatic person or a sweet talker). Listen to the essence or substance of what is being communicated for true value.

Some people only do good to gain fame and power. Some aim for heaven (a temporary resting place before returning to earth for continuing on the path of Self-Realization), rather than aim to realize their eternal life.

Some people use knowledge as power or prestige, or to gain wealth. How many people do you see worshipping knowledge above all else—above ethics, spirit, or compassion. In our modern age, intellectual knowledge is prized over common experience.

Lord Krishna discusses the Vedic notion that the highest, most important knowledge is Self-knowledge, because it is the only permanent knowledge. If a person does not seek this permanence, then of what value is intellectual knowledge. If this knowledge does not provide a lasting experience, what good is it? So Krishna says that even the most spiritual of books are only words unless they provide an eternal experience—that is, a very profound view of the priority of one's relationship with their Soul compared to the relevance of spiritual books. [Verse 42–46]

> *O Arjuna, people who are proud of flowery words are satisfied with the literal Vedic verses, saying, 'this is the only way to interpret the Vedas'. [42]*
>
> *Others, full of desires for selfish, gratification of their senses, see heaven as their highest goal (not realizing it is temporary), and partake in many esoteric scriptural rites just to gain pleasure, wealth, power, and good rebirth. [43]*
>
> *For people who overindulge their sense gratification, acquisition of power and worldly pleasures, their spiritual abilities are diluted, unable to focus on, or feel conviction of purpose to God. [44]*
>
> *The Vedas deal with the three gunas. O Arjuna, be free from attachment to these Gunas; free from pairs of opposites (e.g., heat/cold, pleasure/pain), free from greed and hoarding, be ever steady and self-reliant. [45]*
>
> *For a realized wise person (experiential knowledge), book knowledge of Vedas are of little use, just as well water is of little value when there is fresh lake water at hand. [46]*

Unselfish Giving

Lord Krishna then discusses the relationship between working (including intellectual work) and experiencing eternity (a state of no boundaries, often called a state of nonaction).

The insight is that a person has the right to work to help others or to perform devotional work. But one is not to work to achieve the results (fruits—to get something personal from the action as the reason for working). That would be working for a greedy or selfish motive. So there is something uplifting, something spiritual about working for the sake of working. There is honor in doing your best, honor in selfless work.

This is very similar to the story of the Garden of Eden where God admonishes Adam and Eve to not eat the fruits of the tree of knowledge. God says, avoid trying to get/use/enjoy the fruits of intellect (and stick to the experience of God or God's grace (eg, the garden, the spirit). Because, when you put intellectual knowledge over the innocence of living and enjoying God's world, believing that you can know more than God, then suffering comes.

Krishna continues his reasoning. Working for rewards results in an inferior form of work than does working to help, a more utopian attitude. So even if we do good work but expect some reward in return, that work becomes inferior owing to our lesser intent. (Clearly it is better than not doing good works, but in this context, we are examining various types of good works only.) For example, if the ABC Company decides to work/donate to help feed and clothe the children of poverty, that is good. But if they flaunt their results to look good in their community, then this becomse a something-for-something giving agenda that diminishes their actions.

This is already clear to us when a company has done something dishonorable in the community such as mistreating workers, harming the environment, stealing from investors, etc. The response to being found out is often a PR effort to appear good, such as airing a commercial that highlights the supposed good actions of the company. Many people do see through this façade. However Krishna is talking about something higher, about an already reputable person.

How many of you remember doing something just for doing it? Helping for no reason? Giving without anyone knowing about it, or giving without wanting anything in return? How has that made you feel? Most people I have spoken with say it is the best feeling in the world; better than earning salary. This is what Lord Krishna is talking about.

One wonderful idea Krishna uses is, 'do your best' to do good. That is all a person need to do. Success is in God's hands—so just try your best, but do not try to make something happen. Otherwise the ego gets in the way and proclaims itself The Doer. The value of doing your best, or stated another way, act out of love, removes fear and guilt of failure from the picture. That is all God asks of us.

There is a Vedic tale of how the god Indra tried to hurt the villagers who stopped worshipping him and instead worshipped the one almighty God. Indra hurled a storm of objects down on the village. Lord Krishna lifted a mountain over the village to protect the people. In their gratitude and enthusiasm, the villagers all gathered poles and pushed the mountain up as if they were helping Krishna lift the mountain. They were overjoyed to think they were helping Krishna; but in reality, Krishna was doing all the lifting. So it is in life: we only need to hold our pole up in love and goodness. If it succeeds, it is because God is protecting the people.

Krishna also discusses work on the spiritual level. There are people who do spiritual acts, expecting to receive certain results. For example, they donate to their religious group to get a bronze plaque, or to show off to their friends how much money they have given; they offer prayers to give birth to a male child; or give money or do some charity and expect a favor in return. Lord Krishna warns us to be aware of this kind of egotism.

In the *Upanishads* (another Vedic text), it also says there are two paths to Self-Realization; the lower and higher paths. The first is doing good deeds for some reward (including heaven). The higher path is doing good deeds just for the sake of doing them. The deed itself makes the person feel grateful to be allowed to do the good deed; and that is reward enough for them. It is the higher path that more quickly brings one to Self-Realization.

A deeper, more complex, yet simple idea is discussed here. Devotional action (*bhakti yoga*) frees one from the bonds of this limited relative world to experience the eternal nature of one's Soul. *Bhakti* (Divine love) allows a person to be free from the *guna*s and the various opposites in life. This means that even concepts, such as good and evil, pleasure and pain, winning and losing, are all of little importance, because they are all relative ideas; they do not relate to, nor can they compare to the value of experiencing eternal life.

We can obtain insight into how one becomes unaffected by worldly issues using an analogy of being in love with your spouse. There is the saying that love is blind. People do not see the faults of someone they love. Just as worldly love disengages one's mind from normally troubling issues, so too loving God allows a person to feel freer without being troubled by smaller worldly matters.

The Gunas Defined

According to the Vedic view of creation, there are three fundamental principles that control everything: birth, life, and death. Everything has a beginning, a middle, and an end. The Vedas call these three fundamental principles the three *guna*s: *sattwa* or creation, *rajas* or maintaining, and *tamas* or concluding or ending.

Gunas are seen in our personalities. Some people like to create ideas, food, or companies. Some like to manage and keep an idea or business alive. Still others have the task of removing old, broken, unworkable things, ideas or institutions.

Just as food grows and stays fresh for a time and then becomes inedible, so too are people are born, live, and die. Careers begin and end. Everything in creation is under the influence of these three laws.

Krishna tells us that the secret to peace and spiritual bliss is to go beyond the *guna*s. What does this mean? How can a person go beyond something that controls all material existence? The answer is to switch one's focus from material life to one's spiritual nature. While *sattwa guna* creates all of material life, it is God who has created the *gunas*. In the beginning there was God, and He said, let there be creation. So God created the *gunas* to sustain creation and remove those things that would get in the way of maintaining it.

One may wonder how a person, who is composed of matter, can go beyond the three principles of matter. The answer is that, in this case, we are speaking of the person as the Soul. The person is not merely the matter that houses the Soul, but is the Soul.

Imagine three brothers: Sat, Roger, and Tom Goona. They want to start a computer software company named Goo-Na. It was Sat's idea, and he did all the groundwork to get the company up and going. He got Good Ol' Dad (G.O.D.), venture capitalists, to loan them the startup funds. But since Sat loses interest in the daily activities and likes to move on to create some more dot-com startup companies, Roger was the perfect choice to run the company.

Roger doesn't have much creative sense, so he was happy that Sat started the company; Roger's God-gifts lie in management and organization skills. So he runs the day-to-day operation.

Sat and Roger talked Tom into leaving his job at his salvage company and use his cleanup skills for their new company. Some of Tom's responsibilities will be clearing out old computers, furniture, cell phones, cars, software, and so on, since the company must stay on the leading edge of technology and fashion (to impress the clients). Tom also has the personality to compassionately deal with people when they must be let go. He is also in charge of disbanding parts of companies that their company takes over.

The people who work at Goo-Na have enjoyed their jobs, their salaries support their families, and everything runs smoothly. As the company becomes larger and more powerful, the brothers, human nature being what it is, begin to lose their idealistic focus. Roger becomes power hungry, ie, busy with hostile takeover attempts. Tom has become lazy and sloppy, not clearing out old inventory, not showing up for work, preferring to sit and watch plasma screen TV all day. And Sat, well, he spends all of his time either creating new companies or reading scripture and meditating.

As a result, corporate ethics has slipped and customers are not getting quality products. Creative ideas to serve humanity have fallen by the wayside. Other companies are being harassed where they were previously community partners, and there are even some financial scandals afoot.

There remains one employee, Archie, who joined the company, and who is still inspired by its idealistic mission statement; however, he is quite upset that the company is not allowing him to truly help society. No one listens to his creative ideas. When he tries to talk to any of the brothers, they ignore him. Archie is stuck, trapped by the three brothers. The only way to get out of this predicament is to go over the heads of the Goona brothers. For this, he has to go to the only place that has influence on the Goonas—the Good Ol' Dad (G.O.D.) venture capitalists. G.O.D. holds the purse strings and decides whether to continue funding this company. Since Archie alerted G.O.D. about the loss of vision at Goo-Na, the G.O.D. company may be able to bring integrity, ethics, compassion back into this company by threatening to close them down (ie, stop funding them). As a result of Archie's devotion to helping people, G.O.D. succeeded in putting Goo-Na back on track.

This story gives a brief idea of how the *gunas* work. *Sattwa* creates life. *Rajas* keeps things going. *Tamas* concludes the life cycle. To avoid getting caught up in material life and really know the eternal, nonchanging Divine bliss, Arjuna is advised to go beyond the three *gunas* and to directly seek God.

It may be easier to understand the value of spiritual devotion versus material ideas, through another analogy. A person can have a pile of wood, a box of iron, various tools, some plot of earth. They can even assemble these materials into a living structure. But only when a person, couple or family lives there, does the structure begin to feel like a home, a place filled with love and something beyond a mere object.

The other important point here is that Krishna advises people to not unduly strain themselves to achieve the results of one's action, while simultaneously avoiding under acting or being inactive. Merely sitting doing nothing, keeps one from being involved on an external level only; it does not free the mind and feelings from such desires. There is a myth that the path to Self-Realization is one of renouncing action, but this is incorrect: it is renouncing the desire for the result of action. Not acting does not release the desire for rewards. [Verse 47–53]

> You have the right to fulfill your responsibilities and duties, but not the right to the results (work is its own reward). Neither work for the results of your action, nor be lazy because there is no promise of results to gain. [47]
>
> O Arjuna, be grounded in yoga, perform your duties without attachment, seeing success and failure as the same. [48]
>
> O Arjuna, working for reward is inferior to work that engenders spiritual purpose and closeness to God. So seek refuge in this path of growing spiritual experience. Wretched are those who can only work for rewards. [49]
>
> One who has experienced this spiritual realization is freed from 'good' and 'bad' results in life. For this reason, undertake this path of yoga. Yoga means, skill in action. [50]
>
> The wise who have released their desires for the rewards of action, become free from the yoke of birth and death, and find peace beyond materialism. [51]
>
> When your spiritual awareness pierces the mire of delusion, at that time you will feel indifferent regarding all that you shall ever hear. [52]
>
> When your spiritual intellect has been tossed by the conflicting opinions of the scriptures, then you will become fully established in the Self and attain Self-Realization or oneness with God. [53]

The Signs of a Self-Realized Person

Arjuna then asks how to recognize a person who is Self-realized, and he approaches this from the physical point of view, ie, are there physical traits of a person who is Self-realized. Krishna instantly clarifies that this state does not manifest in a particular physical manner, since it is a spiritual state. He says the Self-Realized person is one who is self-satisfied. Regardless of outer circumstance, they are ok with it; good or bad weather, joyous or sorrowful events, pleasing or threatening situations; no one event impels this person to cause or prevent any situation

Krishna suggests that instead of judging or copying a person's physical mannerisms, it is better emulate their higher values. A person's mannerisms or habits, have little to do with spirit, ethics, or compassion. Steady vision comes from inner values.

The way to achieve such steady vision is to learn to withdraw the senses from worldly involvement. When the body seeks something, the senses often overrule a person's better judgment. For example, craving and eating candy is an example of the sense of taste overriding one's knowledge that white sugar can lead to hyperactivity, high cholesterol levels, or poor digestion. Letting the senses distract us can lead one astray, that is, from the center of one's own inner Soul-home. When one realizes they are so far from home, they can sincerely pray to return to themselves. They then see how much time was lost being sidetracked. Nonetheless, a lesson can be learned. The next time one is tested, they might have greater resolve to prevent becoming sidetracked. [Verse 54–61]

Arjuna said:
O Krishna, what are the signs of a person who is grounded in Self-Realization? How do they speak, sit and walk? [54]

Lord Krishna said:
O Arjuna, when a person is fully satisfied—complete within their Self, completely casting out all mental desires, then they have realized grounded, experiential spiritual wisdom. [55]

One whose mind remains clear even in crisis, out of the grip of pleasures, free of attachment, fear, and anger, is said to be a saint steeped in spiritual wisdom. [56]

One who is free from all attachment neither rejoices over good news, nor is troubled by bad events. They live in the established state of Self-Realization. [57]

When one completely withdraws their senses from material objects, as a turtle retracts its limbs, then their wisdom becomes established in self-contented wisdom. [58]

Through the practice of moderation the embodied Soul can suppress sensory desires, but the desire remains in the heart. All longing vanishes when one experiences the ecstatic love of God. [59]

O Arjuna, the senses are turbulent, for they divert the mind of even the most sincere and wise people seeking to realize what is beyond sensory pleasure. [60]

> *A person of steady wisdom who has succeeded in finding more Divine pleasure from within than from the senses, is able to fix their attention on God. When senses cannot compare to the delight of inner spiritual joy, one has established wisdom. [61]*

Lord Krishna suggests that a person withdraw their senses like a tortoise withdraws their limbs into the shell. This advice alone does not really tell us specifically how to withdraw the senses. There are two general methods for sense withdrawal that work very well to help people gradually reduce the power of the senses and empower the Soul to lure one to the True Eternal Soul.

The first method is to follow a personal Ayurvedic *dosha* food plan and lifestyle. By returning the body, mind, behavior, and spirit to a state of balance, one feels truly a sense of health and vitality that gives new meaning to the word health. As a person becomes truly healthy in this balanced manner, eating something that is not healthy for them, but the senses wants, makes them feel worse, and they naturally reject that food.

For example, a craving for sweets causes the ingestion of white sugar, which has been linked to hyperactivity, and a reduction of energy and nutrition. The best route is to substitute the harmful substance with a good one that will simultaneously satisfy the desire for something sweet and nutritious. In this example, switching to sweets that contain whole cane sugars like sugar cane and maple syrup that retain their inherent nutrients, allows for a more integrated, grounding, and healthy body and mind.

If after a while the person decides to taste a sweet containing white sugar, the harmonious, balanced body will be attacked by the white sugar, and shocking the mind and body causing uncomfortable feelings such as hyperactivity. When the Soul, intuition, or stomach says, 'hey, this is making me sick,' the person will have awakened to the reality that what the senses thought they wanted, the body does not like. The mind and body now take over, stopping activities that harm it. The demands of the senses are illusions, and a balanced *dosha* can dispel the illusion. A person with a balanced constitution (*dosha*), has more control over their senses.

The second way to develop the ability to withdraw the senses is to follow one's life purpose (*dharma*)—doing what one loves to do, that is, doing what comes as second nature. The joy and meaningfulness of such actions unlocks our inner wealth to our awareness. We see that nothing gives us greater pleasure or meaning than to use our God-given talents, and using them to help others, that is, not for selfish reasons. In this state of inner satisfaction and perhaps inner joy, the senses are also satisfied, and so do not cry out for attention.

Both these habits are natural ways a person grows into a state where the senses are satisfied. From these two approaches, a third method automatically arises: gratitude for the sacredness of life as part of a spiritual awakening. Now the Soul is ever more fed through spiritual life, and nothing in the material world can attract our senses as much as the spiritual life.

So the interesting point is that there is no harsh or unnatural forcing of the senses to withdraw, and no complicated intellectual manipulation is required. To ask a person to understand and imagine withdrawing the senses from an abstract theoretical standpoint is virtually impossible. So, too, is it difficult to ask a person to understand the experience of spiritual life if it does not awaken from within. This is the value of these methods of naturally withdrawing the senses, and they will help a person develop the state described by Lord Krishna

Let us return for a moment to the question of how to identify a person who is Self-Realized, and Lord Krishna's answer. Observing human behavior over the years, I have seen clients and acquaintances achieve counterproductive results when trying to judge a person, or determine who is self-satisfied regardless of their circumstances or outer events.

Trying to imagine what traits an ideal person would exhibit suggests possibly preconceived ideas that are not based in reality. Often people tell me their idea of a perfect person is one who never makes a mistake, or who is never angry (always happy). The notion of 'perfection' often relates more to an idea of a mono-emotional or robotic person, that is, someone who is totally devoid of spontaneity, moods, or emotional feeling or reaction; someone in whom there is no happiness or sadness. The opposite is true. A self-satisfied person is one who is most fully emotional, but not for selfish reasons. For example, this person might show sadness—not for their own life—but for the troubles another is undergoing. Or this person might be joyful for the joys of another. With regard to anger, the Vedas distinguish between constructive anger and destructive anger. A realized person is likely to display constructive anger to save someone when they are putting their own life in jeopardy.

Those who base their notions on a faulty premise might begin to compare themselves to an imaginary perfect person who is never angry or who never makes a mistake, who is always attentive, and who is always in a good mood (such false preconceptions may develop from a troubled childhood, imagining a more loving parent). This notion will cause inner conflict. After all, how can you ever feel good about yourself, with all your human flaws, when you will never come close to the assumed perfection of another?

So it is best to not judge yourself against others (real or imagined), and just be the best person you can be. All short-comings melt away when experiencing loving grace of God. Two ways to accomplish this are sadhana (meditation), and thinking less of your personal wants to help others with actual needs.

The Dangers of Letting the Senses Take Control

Lord Krishna describes the mechanics of what happens when the senses go out of control and demand satisfaction. They see an object such as an ice cream cone and demand to have it. They become fixated on the cone as if it were real, as though it could confer everlasting happiness. They long to have the cone, to taste the cone, to gain a lasting inner satisfaction from the cone, which will never happen, even if they taste the ice cream.

This unsatisfied longing causes impatience and irritation that turns into anger. Anger causes the mind to be fully deluded, that is, 'I want that which I don't really want; I want that which I already am; I want a temporary thing instead of an eternal everlasting experience'. In a state of angered delusion, one begins to lose their memory. Did you ever see an angry person so enraged they lose the ability to speak? With the memory impaired, they become deluded, imagining things that never occurred, or forgetting things that did occur. For example, blaming someone for something they never did or for something that never happened. When a person cannot distinguish between fact and fiction, their mental discriminatory faculty becomes damaged, and when a person cannot determine what is real and what is fantasy, their life goes downhill. They have no peace at all, because they seek satisfaction from an irrelevant object.

We can see this from a supposedly 'good' event. Stories abound of people who have won the lottery and become instant millionaires. For one, they sought the prize of ticket, imagining it would bring happiness. And after winning, they become so enamored with the money that they lose touch with their friends and their values. They sometimes find themselves without family, without friends, and soon without money again.

Only a self-satisfied person, one who is satisfied from within, can be at peace. Such persons are comfortable with who they are and so do not become overly upset when they cannot have a material good. They are able to make decisions based on what enhances their inner or emotional life and can distinguish these things from what is fleeting and what detracts from living a pleasant, peace-filled life. These people are called wise. They live their lives on the path of wisdom. [Verse 62–72]

When focused on material objects, a person becomes attached to them. This attachment causes longing for the objects, and this desire generates anger. [62]

From anger arises delusion, which bewilders the memory. With the loss of memory, mental awareness of inner joy is lost. This in turn causes a person to perish. [63]

But those who find greater inner pleasure than from sense pleasures, attains peace and dances gracefully through life free from longings or aversions. [64]

In peace, there is no internal misery, thus allowing the mind to establish itself fully in spiritual joy. [65]

For one with an unsteady mind (i.e., seeking joy from objects instead of spirit) there is no wisdom, meditation or peace. How can the peaceless feel happiness? [66]

Any sense that makes one want to have that pleasure leads the mind away from finding inner pleasure, just as a wind blows a boat off its course. [67]

Therefore, O mighty-armed Arjuna, those whose awareness is tied to their inner joy, are well-protected from the objects of sense pleasure. [68]

For the person who is awake to their inner life (spiritual ecstasy), it always feels like morning, even when it is nighttime outside. What most people call being awake, is considered night for those who have an inner life. [69]

Just as an ocean remains calm while all the rivers flow into it, the self-absorbed saint remains unaffected by sensory objects as they enter them. It is only this type of saint that has no material desires who attains fully established peace (inner joy). [70]

Those who lose their taste for material desires and pleasures find bliss and lives free from false ego and ownership. [71]

O Arjuna, one who realizes this ultimate truth is never again deluded. Even at the end of life, one remains aware of their true eternal nature. [72]

Summary

- Arjuna is confused, having anxiety attacks about life choices. Through this experience, he has learned several important things.

- He is first reminded that people are Souls, not flesh and bones.

- Next he learns people are born to realize their true nature (Soul)

- Life works out favorably when people focus on their life purpose and see life in spiritual terms rather than in material terms. Conversely, life becomes harsh and confusing when a person has a mundane or earthly view.

- Arjuna learns that the secret to life is doing your best to share your love with others, whether they need help, or just to be neighborly. This is all God asks; if you succeed, it is credited to God for He/She/It is the creator of the *gunas*.

- If people see themselves as the doer, the ego blocks them from feeling the love of God, since it is God who does the real work.

- Moreover, it is important to see that helping others is its own reward. Avoid seeking to receive something in return for giving. God is ever giving to the one who sees this realty. Giving without desire for receiving is the highest, fastest way to be closer to God's love.

- Arjuna is reminded that the *gunas* are defined as creation, maintenance, and resolution. All things in creation are governed by the *gunas*. The *gunas* were created by God.

- Lord Krishna talks about realized persons, that they will reveal inner, ethical integrity and have love for God and God's children. And since it is difficult and dangerous to make judgments about others, it is best to work on one's own spiritual path.

- Lord Krishna tells Arjuna that self-discipline of one's senses is essential in remaining balanced and focused on one's spiritual life.

- Arjuna learns that the quality of one's *karma* (loving or harsh actions towards others), returns back to that person. So if one behaves kindly, life returns kindness to them. Unkind behavior brings unkind circumstances in one's life. Like waves on a pond, one's *karma* influences the world and those influences return to the person.

- Lord Krishna explains that reincarnation means the true person is their Soul, not the body. The purpose of life is for a person to realize this reality. Should a body become too infirm to continue the process of Self-Realization, it drops away and the Soul takes a new body to continue on their path of Self-Realization.

- Arjuna learns that compassion in life for others, animals, and nature is essential if one's spiritual life is to feel fully meaningful and palpable.

- Finally, Lord Krishna explains that mere intellectual understanding of something does not make it reality. Only through direct experience can a person truly know something. Just as tasting a food for the first time allows a person to 'know' what that food tastes like—more than just a written description. Intellectual and experiential knowledge are two wings of a bird; both are needed to fly straight.

Modern-Day Discussion

Below are a few concepts discussed in this chapter that I have related to modern life. This is a starting point to inspire the reader of the *Gita* to consider how these ancient verses can offer guidance for modern day-to-day issues in your life. Think about these ideas, discuss them with family, friends, or in your study group.

Karma (Action)

• What happens to *karma* when you do not repay it in this life? Consider *karma* in the context of a spiritual bank account. If you withdraw more than you have, that is, if you create a deficit owing to your actions, words, or thoughts, then you must repay your debt, either by apologizing or incarceration, or some other way. *Karma* adheres to three major principles: (1) the scientific principle that "every action has an equal and opposite reaction"; (2) the religious principle that "as you sow so shall you reap"; and (3) the Golden Rule, "do unto others as you would have them do unto you."

Dharma (Life Purpose)

• Do you know your life purpose or why were you born or what are you on the earth to do? Do you know your own voice or know the message you have come to share? Do you stand up for the less fortunate or helpless? Do you speak up when you feel something is wrong, even at the possible cost of retribution? Have you ever not spoken up when you felt you should have and thus felt remorse, embarrassed, sad, or ashamed? Remember a time when you acted in such a way that you felt your decisions were not based in group think, trends, or modern political correctness; how did you feel from that action? Do you ever act and make choices based on your intuition and not whether the decision will bring you pleasure or pain, acceptance or rejection, winning or losing?

Reincarnation (the Nonchanging Soul)

• When you contemplate your life, note the parts that change: your age, your size, your ideas, your feelings, your beliefs, and so on. What, if anything, has not changed about you? Could it be that you are still the same person inside? That part of you that remains eternally unchanged, immutable, is your Soul, your essence. You are an unchanging Soul.

• Consider the notion that everything in life begins, exists, and then disappears; people are born, live, and then die. So if death is inevitable, but the Soul never dies, why then do we grieve over the dead? Who are we sad for? We don't even know if the departed are comfortable or not, but if we believe they are in God's hands, then a healthy natural grieving process can begin. It is said that if a person can wish the departed Soul well and allow them to move on the next phase of their journey, it will allow both the departed loved one as well as the grieving person to feel lightness and hope. People who have lost a parent, grandparent, their child, or a close friend can more easily understand something of the concept of eternal love. They might still feel the love of the deceased person even though they are no longer in their bodies. Due to the emotional nature of this topic, at first it may be difficult to consider. Write your thoughts in a journal and return to them in a few months to see how you may have grown; maybe you now have a better insight into this issue.

Us and Them

• At the beginning of the battle, Arjuna saw only enemies. But upon leaving his side of the battlefield and getting a closer look at the enemy from the middle of the field, a different perspective, he saw the people behind the us-and-them mentality. This is quite applicable to modern times where there are sharp divisions between Eastern and Western cultures and religions and right and left political parties. This notion can also relate to extremists versus non-extremists and fundamentalists versus moderates. It also relates to organic/holistic/spiritual/vegetarian/ecologists versus those who do not believe in alternative or natural methods.

Angerless Action

- Before Arjuna can fight to defend his race, he must see the reality (with a small 'r') of the situation. He must see that the 'enemy' are people too, some of them beloved friends and family. He must lose his anger as well as his grief, because both are emotions that cloud the mind and prevent it from acting from a centered spirit. From time to time, it is important to consider in one's own life whether you are acting on emotion or from a place of equanimity. In today's world, so many actions and speeches arise out of anger, impatience, and judgement based on other's being less than human (let alone people being your brothers and sisters). From road rage, to dehumanizing political rhetoric and religious demonizing God's other children, anger has deluded our Godly emotions and visions.

Selfless Service

- Consider the times when you have done things expecting something in return, and when you have done things, simply to just help. How do the two situations compare? Contemplate the futility of acting with motives and also not acting at all to try to avoid getting caught up in things. Compare these instances to the times when you have become involved in selfless acts of kindness. Consider times you have not been carried away by your senses—perhaps after *yoga* or meditation, or after eating according to your Ayurvedic diet, or following a sacred lifestyle. Compare such times with situations when you get caught up in life events and become angered and possibly deluded, yelling and saying things that you regret later. What methods do you use to walk ever more on the path of wisdom?

Exercises

To withdraw the senses and walk the Path of Wisdom try to incorporate these harmonious thoughts, words, and actions into your daily life:

1. Follow your Ayurvedic food plan
2. Follow your Ayurvedic lifestyle plan
3. Follow your *dharma* (do what you love to do in life)
4. Pray each day to follow *ahimsa* (not hurt yourself or others in action, words, or thoughts)
5. Help people and give to the earth
6. Find a win-win solution to each situation
7. Have more questions than answers
8. Lead by example
9. Give more than you receive
10. Make decisions that are good for the long term, especially if they are choices that will remain wise for the next seven generations
11. Take walks, as many days as possible per week, and appreciate the nature around you.
12. Note the harmony when it is there and appreciate it; cultivate it when it isn't there. Use *Vastu Shastra* and Feng Shui in your home and office to enhance the harmony
13. Try *yoga* or *tai chi*
14. Spend some time in nature (woods, water, desert, a park, or your garden) each week
15. Take time each week to play music or listen to music, or involve/expose yourself to the arts (for example, poetry, dance, sculpting, painting)
16. Each day, leave some space in your life for God to fill
17. Talk to God each day, even if for a few minutes. Share your feelings, questions, and ask for guidance to grow closer and feel the palpable love of God

Krishna advises people to find their eternal Soul,
beyond reincarnation: the never-ending cycle of life and death

Chapter 3
How to Attain Peace Through Action

In the last chapter, Lord Krishna gave advice about the value of the '*yoga* of wisdom', saying: 'Developing inner joy is better than working for outer pleasures.'

Ajuna now asks why Krishna is asking him to act, more-over to kill. He asks an intelligent question:
'It seems as if you are making contradictory statements. If you say wisdom is superior to action, why do you ask me to act, to fight in this horrific war?'

Lord Krishna reminds Arjuna that freedom from the bondage of actions doesn't come from stopping action, neither does perfection (Self-Realization) develop through non-action. This is because life is ever inactive owing to the three gunas (*sattwa*, purity or creation; *rajas*, activity or maintaining; *tamas*, stopping of action or destruction). The three *gunas* are always active.

Even when the body is seemingly inactive, the heart keeps pumping, and the blood circulating. Thus, the inner body remains continually active. Stopping action does not really stop all action. Moreover, the mind is always active. If a person does not eat a candy bar, but secretly desires one, they are still enslaved to their senses even though appearing to have broken the hold on the taste buds.

When a person feels balanced, and then eats unhealthy food, it causes them to become imbalanced. Only then will they feel repulsed by unhealthy food. Mastery of the senses occurs when you are no longer ensnared by foods and other sensory impressions. Although this is a difficult task, it has been found that by following one's Ayurvedic food plan (one that balances), feeling greater health from within one's eternal Soul, begins to take precedence over a temporary and possibly harmful sensory pleasure. This is why Lord Krishna says action is superior to inaction.

So only when a person can engage in the world and not be enslaved by it, or as Lord Krishna says, to perform action without attachment, can one say they have attained the *yoga* of wisdom. It is not a question of 'whether or not to act. It is more a question of acting without attachment or enslavement by the senses. [Verse 1–9]

Arjuna said:
O Krishna, if the spiritual-mental awareness is considered better than action, why are you are you asking me to engage in this horrific action? [1]

These seem to be conflicting words that have caused me mental confusion. Please clarify which will allow me to attain the highest benefits. [2]

Lord Krishna said:
O sinless one, this world has both paths previously described by Me. The path of wisdom is for those with an affinity to more intellectual thinking, and the path of work is for those with more natural affection for activity. [3]

A person can neither become free from actions nor attain perfection simply by not performing action. [4]

No one can exist without some action always taking place. All of nature is ever compelled to be active by its design (due to the action of the gunas). [5]

Anyone who has controlled the five sense organs, yet is thinking about sensory objects, is fooling themselves and being hypocritical. [6]

Yet, O Arjuna, anyone who has mental control over their senses, follows the path of action without attachment; they can control their sense organs (organs of action). [7]

Therefore, perform your allotted responsibilities because this is better than forsaking obligations. If all activity stopped, the body could not function. [8]

O Arjuna, the entire world is bound by actions, except for actions that are offered to God (yajna). Therefore, do your duty while being free from attachment. [9]

Abundance Consciousness

Lord Krishna also examines (in a very abstract way) the notion of how it is better to give than to receive. Giving has various levels; in the world, it might relate to giving time, material possessions, or love. On an intimate level, it would mean saying a prayer over your food (giving thanks to God for the food) and offering all things you own to God, before using them to help humanity. It can mean giving all your ownership of all things, feelings, and thoughts to God as well. The idea of human ownership is said to be fictitious, since it is God who gives all things to people.

In this context, Krishna says he has given certain responsibilities to his angels (*devas*) for them to manage (give) to others. Offering or giving requires relinquishing the ego's notion of ownership of things. When a person has no particular desire to own something (or someone), their desires become spiritual desires, for example, the desire to help humanity. So without holding on to the objects or feelings, they are given freely in a positive, helpful spirit.

Food that has been prayed over becomes *prashad* or holy food—the remnants of food tasted by God—and so upon eating, the food purifies the individual's body, mind, and spirit. However, those who horde food, who are not grateful for the bounty, the ego energy grows, and the food becomes the energy of greed.

Conversely, one who does not covet is never lacking; one who accepts all things as a part of the eternal energy of God cannot be without, because how can eternity lack? We see examples of abundance everywhere in nature. Birds and fish seem to always find food. Why wouldn't God provide the same system of abundance for humans?

It is only when human's ego (greed) gets in the way that it blocks the abundance from being seen and received; or when humans want what they don't have—when they value what is rare over what is given in abundance—the opposite of supply and demand economy. Being grateful for what God supplies in abundance is a way to realize life in fullness. Undue effort is then not required.

In the book, *Yoga Vani*: *Instructions for the Attainment of Siddhayoga*, by Swami Shankar Purushottam Tirtha, the author says that God guarantees to those who think of God and serve God's children will always find they have the basic necessities in life; they never have to doubt or come out of the mindset of serving and giving to others. Similarly, if we plant one seed of a marigold flower, it produces hundreds of flowers for a 6 to 8-month cycle. As each flower dies, it leaves behind hundreds of seeds. So by planting one seed, Mother

Nature gives back millions of seeds. From this we can see a parallel. By doing one healthy/natural thing for yourself or for others, Mother Nature gives back a million-fold. This is how creation is set up. Those who give and live in natural harmony grow in health and peace and God-love. The process goes on by itself, set up by God.

Those who try to make the impermanent material world their own (that is, who greedily hoard), cannot experience the everlasting. The Bible says Eve lost her faith in God and chose to taste the fruit of intellectual knowledge, as if she could know something as worthy as knowing God. So in her doubt, she stopped giving and took, and thus cut herself off from her Divine life. But those who are aware of their inner eternal Soul and are not swayed by outer material life and those who do not work to meet their own selfish ends, can flow easily with nature and find that it takes less effort to achieve what they must.

These days some people define abundance theory as 'you can get whatever you want in life'. But Lord Krishna offers a deeper insight into the true meaning of abundance; you *are* everything, because at its essence everything is Soul. So there is no need to 'need' or want—Soul is ever-present, everywhere. Even viewing this from a material viewpoint, God knows what you need, is ever supplying what you need in abundance, so there is no need to desire for yourself. The result of this insight is freeing. Then one naturally begins to think of helping others from what runneth over in their life.

You might think abundance theory describes the land of milk and honey. Reading accounts of indigenous peoples such as native American Indians during the time of Columbus, we see this is how they lived. Families were always together, living, loving, connected with the earth. Gathering food was a family event. Children could sit on parent's shoulders and pick fruit off the trees. Although it was work, interactions with family lessened the effort required.

There is a natural life-spirit cycle; offer all you do, say, and think to God and for the benefit of others. In this way, you and all will be sustained. If you do not seek to sustain others in this way, your senses will be temporarily gratified, but inner and eternal joy will remain elusive because you have cut yourself off from your inner eternal abundance.

There is an interconnectedness between humans, animals and nature. The fish eat the flies at the surface of the water, the birds eat the fish who rise to the surface, and so on. There is a sacred interconnectedness among all living things. In this verse, Krishna unveils the very essence of all cycles—offering action to God, or living for others instead of for selfish motives. Selfless living is what propels the positive life-growth cycle. Flies are offered to fish, and fish to birds. Humans can feed, or feed off other humans. We have the ability to choose to be selfless and offer our love and lives for the betterment of humanity, and this in turn betters us.

Verse 17 reveals the unlimited abundance of bliss or contentment that is within each person. When this reservoir is discovered, our external-based desires for happiness vanish because the eternal and most blissful inner joy supersedes any temporary and limited joy obtained through difficult effort. So Lord Krishna says the person who is devoted to their inner eternal Soul is satisfied with their inner self, is content with their inner self (without longing for anything external); for that person, there is nothing to do [Verse 10–17]

In the beginning of creation, Brahma created all beings as an offering to God, saying, 'by this offering shall you prosper; through offerings, all that is desirable shall be bestowed upon you. [10]

By this sacrificial offering (yajna), the heavenly hosts (devas) are pleased, and in turn shall bless you to obtain the highest blessings. [11]

The offering (yajna) to the Almighty satisfies the heavenly hosts (devas) and blesses you with all the desired necessities of life. People who enjoy life's blessings without first offering them to God, are called thieves. [12]

Spiritual or righteous people who eat the remnants of the offering are freed from all sins; but people who prepare food for themselves, eat sin. [13]

Creatures come into being from food; food is produced from rain, rain comes as a result of the offering (yajna) to God, and the offering occurs due to karma (action). [14]

Understand that actions originate from the Vedas, and the Vedas arise from the eternal, Almighty. Thus, the all-pervading Brahman is ever established in the performing of offerings unto God. [15]

> *O Arjuna, people who do not partake in this cycle live in sin, wasting their lives enslaved by their need for sense gratification. [16]*
>
> *Those who remain ecstatic and self-content within themselves; activity doesn't exist for them. [17]*

While writing this section, the topic of nirvana (the land of milk and honey) arose during a conversation with a student. She said she did not want to live in nirvana since she defined it as 'not having to do anything'—she wanted a life of challenges and helping others. She held a common myth or mistaken (myth-taken) definition of nirvana.

Lord Krishna says the message in this chapter is to act with wisdom (inner reflection) and be involved with devotional work and helping others. This in itself will help a person feel closer to the Divine—the true definition of nirvana. But the Western notion of success involves endings such as winning a game. When you win, the games ends, and there is nothing to do. In this context, then, achieving nirvana would be akin to having reached the end of the game, at which point you are put out to pasture. Nothing can be further from the truth. Nirvana is a life that is full, not empty, for it is at that point that one experiences living and acting in full harmony with the Divine.

Another misconception about nirvana or Self-Realization is that one becomes a zombie, emotionless, without thought, feeling, or life. Again, it is quite the opposite. One is fully awake, fully alive, and fully sensitive. It is ironic that the state of natural balance and awakened consciousness would be thought of as something artificial or unnatural.

Lord Krishna says that by accepting that Almighty God as the owner and provider for all humans and creatures, there is nothing to gain by doing, and nothing to lose by not doing; one need not depend on any person Dependence on God alone allows a person to be enthralled in this nirvana or garden of Eden.

Lord Krishna tells Arjuna that this is the reason why it is best to be detached from selfish desires; just try to help people from love (*bhakti yoga*):

> *Help for no reason other than it feels good to help.*
> *Don't help to get, God alone is the giver.*
> *Don't help out of fear, pride, or fame, you won't be freed.*

Fear and pride serve the dish of doubt and cause you to disbelieve in abundance; fear evokes the acrid taste of emptiness (not receiving), and pride reveals a sweet gluttony that something additional is needed to feel good about yourself, thus resulting in low self-esteem and scarcity instead of self-worth and abundance. Low self-esteem cooks more dishes for fear and pride to serve, causing a cycle of overeating doubt.

Helping is the highest calling. The fullest expression of helping is to teach through example. So when a person is full of the eternal abundance of their inner Soul, they are at peace. They are able to accept life and act appropriately, come what may. When they help, it is in response to their cup running over; they are moved by compassionate joy. When they are not acting, they still are feeling the abundance and enjoyment just the same. Either way, awakening to the experience of inner abundance finds one in Divine rapture (*sat chit ananda*); beyond feeling fullness, one feels Divine glory. The person who shines with such joy is infectious, and others around them spontaneously beam with the same radiant bliss.

The interesting point is that two people can be helping (for example, feeding the poor), one may be thinking, 'this will look good on my resume'; the other is overflowing with the abundance of inner self, God-love. It is the second person who is truly helping the people. Their love-abundance runneth over and everyone around them bathes in a warm loving smile; their Souls are touched and freed by the freed Soul of the truly giving person.

Divine Prayer

'Lord, give all your Divine ecstasy, give all your love; let it flow through me unimpeded—washing flooding out into the world over and through the people, saturating, inciting Divine delight of God in all.'

Krishna says,
Help out others out of a sense of loving service. The great Souls of this earth attained salvation by this method. The people follow the actions of leaders—useful or non-useful actions; so it is important to set a good example for the masses.

It may be easier to understand the notion of what is 'action without care for results' through examples of action with and without a desired reward.

Action Desiring Reward	Action Desiring No Reward
Prayer : 'I pray for money', or 'for a child', or 'for health'. This is a prayer—a good thing—but done for a desired result	Prayer: 'I pray for the best possible result for people and the creation—whatever God/spirit wishes'; or 'I pray that all people do not harm themselves, anyone or anything.'
I will donate to your campaign if you in turn put me on your staff (or enact legislation favorable to our company)	I will donate to this cause (ideally anonymously) because I believe in what you are doing for people, nature, etc.
I will help you if you promise to help me when I need help	I'll help you (just because it feels good to help)
I'll donate to your charity if you put my name on a plaque	I'll donate to your charity (ideally anonymously), just because I believe in what you are doing
Our company won't pollute the environment if you give us a tax incentive	Our company does not want to pollute and will not pollute because we can find a way to profit in a win-win situation

Lord Krishna then says that even He—who has no need of anything since He is everything and created everything—even He acts
unceasingly trying to do good out of His love for His children. He
says, if he does not act, the people also would also not act and the
world would perish. Therefore, the wise must act to help humanity
without attachment to desires. [Verse 18–26]

---

*Such a person has nothing to gain from action and nothing to lose from inaction, and is
entirely self-reliant and self-sufficient. [18]*

*Therefore, remaining unattached, continually perform you dutiful actions. It is through these
acts you achieve the highest good. [19]*

*Through such actions, King Janaka and other (great souls) realized complete perfection. For
the sake of helping the world, you also should discharge your responsibilities. [20]*

*How a great person conducts themselves, the average people follow. Whatever example
they set, the people follow. [21]*

*O Arjuna, in these spiritual, heavenly, and material worlds, there is no prescribed responsi-
bilities for Me, and nothing to gain. Still I continue my assigned duties. [22]*

*O Arjuna, if I do not unceasingly carry out my duties, people would follow my example in all
areas of their life. [23]*

*O Arjuna, if I do not execute my responsibilities, the worlds would crumble. The castes would
become confused, and all beings would be destroyed. [24]*

*O Arjuna, as the ignorant are attached to the rewards of work, so the wise act without per-
sonal motive, but to help the world. [25]*

*The foolish, attached to results of action, are not to be confused; the wise are thus advised
to engage in their dutiful or righteous action. [26]*

But Krishna notes it is not for the person who comprehends this to
confuse those who are not ready to understand this insight. Thus,
this information should not be forced on others. The wise, however,
are to focus on their Soul, acknowledging that all action is in the
hands of God, and try to help out of love (not out of hope for some
attainment, honorable recognition, or grief to gain something).

Whatever gifts you have been given, you must use them in the world.
For Arjuna, who is a warrior and one who upholds righteousness, his
path is to help those who are being threatened with genocide by his

cousin. Krishna says those who try to help in this manner, faithfully, devotedly, with unflinching heart become free from the bondage of the senses and ego and can thus attain Self-Realization.

However, He cautions that those who find fault with his teaching and do not follow this path of wise action and devotional helping will be deluded and ruined.

For the wise, this will be their natural path. Lord Krishna says it is better to follow one's own life-purpose path though flawed, than to follow another's path. It is only by living your own life that you will become free.

> *I shall be telling this with a sigh*
> *Somewhere ages and ages hence:*
> *Two roads diverged in a wood, and I,*
> *I took the one less traveled by,*
> *And that has made all the difference*

The American poet, Robert Frost called this 'the road less traveled.' When we look and see everyone walking one way, but we are called to another separate path, called to create yet a new path, it may seem unfair, or lonely. On that isolated path, one might face lack of external recognition and validation. In addition, others not called to that path might attempt to talk you out of walking your path. Often it is our loving family, who, with the best intentions, advise us to follow a path that has already been tread because they can only see paths already trodden.

Another American poet, Henry David Thoreau, said:

> *If a man does not keep pace with his companions,*
> *perhaps it is because they hear a different drummer.*
> *Let them step to the music they hear,*
> *however measured or far away.*

Lord Krishna warns that following another's path is fraught with danger. [Verse 27–35]

The ego deludes the mind into believing 'I am the doer'. The gunas, born of prakriti (nature) perform all actions. [27]

But, O mighty-armed, the knower of truth, who understands the functioning of the gunas and the results of action of the senses, witnesses the senses engaged in sense objects, and so doesn't become attached to them. [28]

Those with perfected insight are not to confuse the people who are deluded and therefore attached to the gunas (senses). [29]

Without ego or desire for gains, surrender all action to Me; set your mind firmly focused on the Self; thus becoming free from the fever of grief, and fight. [30]

People who continually follow these teachings of Mine with full faith and devotion, become freed from the bondage of being affected by the results of actions. [31]

But, those who find fault with my teachings and do not follow the advice, they are deluded and devoid of any true inner knowledge or spiritual awareness. [32]

Even the wise act according to their nature; all beings follow their own nature. What can repression accomplish? [33]

The sense objects cause attraction and aversion of the senses. People should try to not be controlled by their sense desires as they divert one from finding their true path (inner eternal bliss). [34]

It is better to perform one's own life-purpose though flawed, than to live that of another's. It is better to die on one's own path than to live according to another person's life purpose; the purpose of another is full of danger [35]

Arjuna then asks Krishna,
'What power is it that causes a person to act in ways that even they don't wish to act?'

Krishna says,
Unfulfilled or obstructed desire causes anger. It is created from *rajas guna* (excess action). This craving is never satisfied, and causes self-harming action. This desire envelopes wisdom like dust hides the mirror. The eternal Soul is hidden by this desire. It is the constant enemy of the wise. Desire hides in the senses, mind, and intellect, and afflicts wisdom. This is why Lord Krishna advises to subdue the senses. The way to become free from these bonds of desire are through meditation, prayer, following one's life purpose, following one's Ayurvedic foods and lifestyle, and trying to not harm anyone or anything (in action, words, and thoughts). The senses are stronger than the body, the mind is stronger than the senses, the intellect is

stronger than the mind, and the Soul is strongest of all. So freeing oneself from desires can be achieved with willpower, perseverance, and with the help of gentle, natural habits of meditation, lifestyle, and monitoring one's thoughts, words, and deeds. [Verse 36–43]

Arjuna said:
O Krishna, what impels a person to commit sin against their own will, as if compelled by force? [36]

Lord Krishna said:
It is unfulfilled desire, turning into anger, born of Rajas Guna (passion); know this craving to be insatiable and the greatest sin; it is the most formidable enemy of the world. [37]

Just as fire is hidden by smoke, dust hides a mirror, the womb hides the embryo, so the Self is hidden by desire. [38]

O Arjuna, wisdom (inner joy) is hidden by the unappeasable fire of desire; it is the constant enemy of the wise. [39]

The senses, mind, and intellect are the seats of desire; through these organs desire deludes the embodied Soul and covers its wisdom. [40]

Therefore O Arjuna, first control your senses; destroy this sinful desire, for it is the destroyer of wisdom and Self-Realization. [41]

The senses are superior (to the body), mind is superior to the senses, and the Soul (atman) is superior to the mind. [42]

O mighty-armed, by knowing Soul is superior to intelligence, steady the mind by Soul awareness and conquer the unappeasable enemy in the form of desire. [43]

Summary

- Self-Realization (realizing inner peace) does not come from in-action, but from lovingly sharing, helping others, and giving of yourself

- God's abundance is there for all creatures. So there is no need to think selfishly of how to get and do things for yourself. Rather, live a life in balance, devotedly, serving others (*bhakti*) and your basic needs will be met

- Desireless action means giving of yourself and acting for the benefit of others. It is based in abundance consciousness—where one feels their cup runs over. Conversely, desire-based action is based in selfish desires. It is due to, and causes feelings of lacking abundance

Exercises: Abundance

- Look at the animals in nature; do you see how they are generally provided for or find food without undue effort? [yes, there are exceptions to the rule]. Generally do you see there is enough food for the birds, fish, etc., and how there is an interwoven layering of life so all animals have food?

- Now review your life patterns. Can you find times when somehow things come to you when you needed them most-maybe you're not sure how it happened. Maybe some money came in the mail just when you needed extra funds, or an idea came to you to finish your report just before the deadline. Do you find that when you are involved with events that are more to help others rather than for your own personal desires, abundance appears more often if not every time?

- If you do see this pattern of abundance in you life when you are selfless, then develop a strategy to gradually become even more selfless. Obviously you need to support yourself and family, but you can choose a career that is more beneficial to people and nature. If you are realistically able to transform even an extra hour or so a day to more selflessness, do you see the increased abundance growing in your life even more than before? Does your inner contentment and life energy feel yet fuller? If so, continue to expand your selfless outlook and actions.

Abundance: from one seed comes thousands

Chapter 4
The Eternal Path to God

Lord Krishna begins the chapter documenting that He has taught this *yoga* wisdom to various royal sages throughout history. He calls it imperishable *yoga* because God is eternal; thus, it provides the wisdom to realize that God is also eternal. From time to time and over time, the wisdom can become lost. It must then be taught anew to other generations. At this time, Krishna is teaching this same wisdom to Arjuna.

Avatars

To explain the gain and loss of wisdom, Krishna says,
Whenever there is a decline in virtue and a rise of vice, Almighty God comes to earth, taking a form to protect good people and destroy the evil ones. In this way, *dharma* (virtue, goodness, love of spirit/God) is restored.

In Vedic culture (the Hindu religion), the form God assumes is called an avatar. Past avatars included Ramakrishna, Rama, Krishna, Shankara, and a variety of animals. Thus it is that Hindus also accept Jesus and Buddha as avatars. These avatars come to earth and live exemplary lives--usually bearing the greatest of hardships--yet always remaining true to *dharma*, ethics, and virtue. These avatars are spiritual role models or mentors who teach us how to live virtuously even amid the harshest challenges.

Now another aspect of an avatar is also discussed. Since God or spirit is in all people and all things, then all people and things are avatars. Then if a person can see the Holy Spirit in rocks, trees, people, and so on, it can be said that they see God or spirit in all things. Once the great saint Ramakrishna was asked if indeed he was the avatar of Rama and Krishna. He answered that for those who believe in diversity, he is the avatar of both past avatars. For those who see all people and things as God, then all people and things are avatars. And we are God as much as Ramakrishna is.

Krishna says people who understand the nature of these Divine births and His virtuous actions as an avatar, see themselves as that same eternal spirit. Thus, they attain the goal of their life—Self-Realization; they do not need to be reborn. Reincarnation would not be necessary. Such people become free from fear, anger, and all forms of attachment. They are absorbed in the love of God. Taking refuge in God, they have gone through the fire of wisdom and been purified into eternal life.

Other religions have the same or similar view of reincarnation. Judaism believes by naming their children with the same first letter as a departed relative, that relative's Soul is reborn. Some forms of Buddhism (eg, Tibetan Buddhists) believe in the reincarnation of the Soul. Other sects do not use the term Soul, but call it 'life' (beyond time and space, beyond inside and outside, no life or death). So Buddhists say there is no reincarnation, but rebirth of 'life.' Semantically, it is the same idea; it is just using different names. Other mystical religions also believe in reincarnation. [Verse 1–10]

Lord Krishna said:
I taught this science of imperishable yoga to Surya who taught it to his son Vaisvastu Manu, who taught it to his son, King Ikshvaku. [1]

Thus, the lineage of sage-kings learned this science. O Arjuna, through a long duration of time, this science of Self-Realization became lost in this world. [2]

Today, that same ultimate yogic science has been again taught by Me to you, because you are my devotee and friend. [3]

Arjuna said:
I don't understand; you were born after Surya, how could you be his teacher? [4]

Lord Krishna said:
O Arjuna, you and I have had many births. I remember them all, but you do not. [5]

Though I am timeless, unborn and imperishable, and the Lord of all creation, I birth myself into a living being by my own internal mysterious power. [6]

O Arjuna, whenever righteousness diminishes and unrighteousness starts to prevail, at those times I manifest in living form. [7]

I birth myself from age to age to protect the good, destroy the evil-doers, and to re-establish dharma (virtue and spirituality). [8]

> O Arjuna, those who understand My spiritual birth and purposes, upon leaving their body, are not born again; they attain unto Me. [9]
>
> Freed from attachment, fear, and anger, fully absorbed in Me, taking refuge in Me, attain My divine love (ecstasy). [10]

Just One God

Verse 11 is a wonderfully profound statement by Lord Krishna. He says that however a person worships God, God answers them in kind. There are many paths people follow to reach God.

> However people worship Me, I fulfill those desires. O Arjuna, all mankind follows My path. [11]

Every major religion says there is only one God. Here, Krishna clearly says that He accepts all paths to the one God. So if one reads Jesus saying, 'I am the Way', one might also conclude, in an open-hearted interpretation, that Jesus might be speaking figuratively. The same with other religions, each says, 'God is the Way'. But there is no actual statement that God *must* be in this sole form for people to worship. That would be a literal interpretation. If God is truly all-loving, wouldn't He be accepting of all paths He created in the first place? Each path has its own rules and rituals; heavens and hells, falling and redemption, but all speak of the one eternal God or spirit. This verse then demonstrates full acceptance of all paths to God. If religions could celebrate their similar goal, we could avoid religious wars.

In verse 12, Krishna says that those who long for worldly success worship the gods, but that worldly success is more quickly attained by actions. There is a difference between God giving a devotee the basic necessities for their family to survive without undue stress, and a person praying for untold wealth. Here, Krishna is speaking of the person desirous of excess worldly wealth. So in these two verses, He distinguishes between reaching God and attaining worldly success.

Krishna further clarifies who God is in relation to actions and gods. He says that God created all things and actions (qualities/*gunas* and *karma*), He is not the doer; He is unmoving, unchanging. Any action cannot pollute or move His eternal nature. Those who experience this reality are not bound by their actions, that is, they do not act out of personal desires such as fame, fortune, or power.

So we see that God has given options to all people; they can worship and attain Him, or they can aim for untold wealth. But to truly know God, you must go beyond all action and doing to realize Oneness with the eternal, unbounded Soul. [Verse 12]

> *Those who long for worldly success worship the demigods; success comes quickly through actions. [12]*

Dispelling the Myth of the Caste System

Lord Krishna says He created the four-fold caste system. The four castes include the religious class (*Brahmins*), the soldiers (*Kshatriyas*), business class (*Vaishyas*), and the servant class (*Shudras*). The religious class is said to represent the spiritual qualities of goodness, ethics, virtue, serenity, and other *sattwic* attributes. The warrior class is said to represent goodness (*sattwa*), passion/desire, and dullness (*rajas* and *tamas*, respectively). The servant class is said to represent dullness, ignorance, and inertia (*tamas*).

Now these terms have become misused, misinterpreted, and consequently highly inflammatory. What was once a horizontal division of labor, where people worked in areas most suited to their nature (eg, tall, strong people were the defenders of good; nature lovers worked the land, etc); evolved into a judgmental, condescending vertical system, where the priests claimed to be most superior and the servants were considered 'untouchable.' Even the notion of ignorance was distorted, labeling as ignorant the people whose love and devotion was all they needed in this world. They cared not for intellectual understanding, since they had found Divine wisdom. Indeed, intellectual ignorance became known as something that prevented one from knowing God. This is incorrect.

In reality, each caste depends on the other for support. The tall and strong were the defenders. The physically weak and philosophically oriented prayed for the community. The nature lovers farmed the land, the shopkeepers kept the community stocked with needed supplies. Caste exemplified nature's interdependency of peoples. [Verse 13]

> The four divisions (castes) of humans was created by Me according to the differences in people's qualities, actions, and abilities. While I am the creator of this world, know Me as the changeless non-doer. [13]

Action, Inaction and Detachment

As mentioned earlier, actions do not affect the eternal, nonmoving, non-object, absolute form of Krishna, nor does He desire any rewards of action such as wealth, fame, or power. Those who know this by experience also are not bound by action. Thus, wise persons act to help others without seeking a reward for their help.

Now there is a subtler form of attachment and action. There are those who begin by helping others, but later may start to crave the honor they receive from helping others rather than just helping others without their knowing you have helped. So true detachment from action—action without desiring a reward—is difficult to achieve.

The notions of action and inaction are difficult to understand even for wise people. Krishna distinguishes the difference between actions to become free from those which enslaves the mind, body, and Soul. He says there is Right action, Unlawful action, and Inaction.

A common story in India illustrates detached giving. When a person is helped by a saint, the person asks, 'How can I thank you, how can I repay you?" To which saints generally reply, 'You can thank me by helping someone else; pass it on."

[Verse 14–17]

Actions never affects Me, nor do I have any desires for the rewards of actions. Those who understand Me in this way are also not ensnared from actions. [14]

Knowing this, the ancient enlightened ones still performed their duties. Thus, you too must dispense your responsibilities as did your wise ancestors. [15]

Even the wise are bewildered regarding what is action and inaction. So, I will teach you about action that leads to liberation from inauspicious matters. [16]

You need to understand the natures of 'right (harmonious) action', unnatural action, and inaction. The nature of karma is very difficult to understand. [17]

Vision of the Wise

People who realize that even while acting (involving the movement of mind, body, senses), the Soul remains still—eternal. The sages recognize wisdom in a person who realizes this—for such wise people have had the fire of wisdom burn away the illusion that the Soul (the true person) is acting. These people have gone through their trials by fire.

By not caring for reward and helping others merely to help, one becomes content and self-sufficient (ie, never needing to depend on others to feel contentment or happiness) Acting to help, knowing the Soul is not doing anything; thus, taking credit or pride in the action is not possible.

A parent, for example, loves their child and tries to guide them to live their life while growing into adulthood. A wise parent would allow the child to find themselves by trial and error, and once the child knows what truly brings them a sense of fulfillment and life purpose, lovingly encourage them on their path.

Now, a parent who is not yet wise, a parent who themselves has not found fulfillment or purpose in life, may try to manipulate the child to live out the parent's unfulfilled dreams. The parent may push the children for success so they will take care of the parent. Or a parent may be overly attached and co-dependent on the child to allow them to find themselves or learn through trial and error. All these are examples of caring for the results of one's actions, and being unable to be detached from a situation.

Krishna says that a person can be freed from longing for something, since people are already everything (ie, the eternal omnipresent); one automatically has the ability of self-control. There is no notion of ownership or possession, because every object and person are a part of the eternal 'is-ness.' Things and people just are. Thus, money exists; it is neither yours nor mine, it is a part of the eternal whole. The Soul does not gain from fame or money, and it is not lessened without them. [Verse 18]

It is the wisest of people who see inaction in action and vice versa. They are established in wisdom, harmoniously and dutifully performing all their actions. [18]

Detachment, Gratitude, and Contentment: Keys to Living in Harmony

A person becomes content with whatever comes effortlessly—as life unfolds, they accept what befalls them, because it does not touch their Soul, their Self.

Here is an example. Owing to early-life circumstances, a person had to stop school to support his family. Over the decades, he got married, raised children, and supported the children even when they got married and had their own children.

Years later, the children are adults and able to work and support the extended family (grandparents, parents, and children). And the person once again thought about things he wished to do with his life: study, spend more time on spiritual matters and less on business matter, especially now that his mind was becoming increasingly less focused on business.

Instead of seeing this as an opportunity, he became desperate with his failing business powers, trying harder, forcing, embarrassed, and making bad decisions just to bring home a salary, but instead, losing more money owing to rash decisions.

The more he forced a decision, the more troubles he got into—financially and then health-wise. He found himself in the hospital many times, incurring more expense to the family.

Then he began to pity himself, thinking, 'I am not worthy, I am becoming a burden to the family.' So swinging from the extreme of irrational action to inaction and lowering self-esteem, this person has bounced back and forth with no constructive vision.

With growing insecurity, he lashed out at his family as a pitiable way to feel some power. Projecting frustrations, he criticized everything the children were doing; no work was good enough because the salary was never enough to instantly relieve the financial hole he dug for himself. Everything became about getting big money in a quick way.

This story is a recipe for disaster. This person nearly destroyed the health, love, and well being of himself and his family, all because he was enslaved by the desire to achieve the goal—in this case, money—and all because he could not accept letting go; he could not accept a change in life to a more meaningful life-purpose. This person saw himself as the doer—doing for a desired result—and could not let go even when, after years of repeating this harmful behavior, he achieved the same unsuccessful outcomes. Slowly, this person began to realize and tried to appreciate their situation, spending more time in spiritual pursuits (eg., sadhana, reading scriptures) and feeling more gratitude for his life.

There is a modern-day story relating Lord Krishna's ideas that humans are not the doer. Act in mind, body, and senses to help others, knowing that you (the Soul) is not doing the acting. See God as the doer, and accept how life unfolds when you try your best. In the story of the unsuccessful man, he tried being the 'doer.' Ego kept luring him to be the hero. When that failed, ego lured him to feel he was the goat, unsuccessful. The middle path says that you must be grateful for your God-given talents, use them wisely, and see how it is God that works through you to accomplish acts. The result is a fulfilled, grateful person—detached from the acts, detached from the results—content from within and not because of external circumstances.

There is an expression, if at first you don't succeed, try, try, again. However, success should not be sought from the point of view of ego. Lord Krishna says, '*success is in the trying*'. To prevent ego from taking over, a person must be detached and open-minded to realize when their ego is out of control and driving them to ruin.

There is another saying: when one door closes, another opens. Accept it when a door has closed and look for new doors to be opened to you. This is a basic recipe for a contented, spiritual life. This teaching clarifies the myth some have about contentment and meditative life as an inactive life. The inaction is internal, when one's Soul realizes it is the true non-acting self amidst daily life.

The person who is detached from getting and who is liberated from the notion of being the doer, and from receiving or earning fame and fortune, will work to help others and in this way melt away their past *karma* (actions). [Verse 19–23]

The sages call that person wise whose actions are done without desire for reward, and whose actions are burned by the fire of wisdom. [19]

The person who, losing the desire for the rewards of action, is ever-content, and self-reliant, all while fulfilling their responsibilities, acts not. [20]

Free from desire and ownership, self-controlled, this person is not stained by sin from performing action to sustain life. [21]

Satisfied with what life brings without undue effort, undisturbed by life's dualities, lacking envy, and even-minded in success and failure, even while acting is not entangled. [22]

The person who is no longer attached to materialism, is liberated, and whose mind and heart have penetrated wisdom, who performs all action as an offering to God, all their karma dissolves. [23]

Different Forms of Sacrifice (Selfless Service)

The highest form of sacrifice is to let go of personal desires, and in fact, all mundane desires, dedicating all actions to God. Thinking with each action, *Thy will be done*, is the quickest way to Self-Realization, that is, feeling God's love fully.

It is said that the actor (eternal Soul) is *Brahman*; the action (sacrificial offering) is *Brahman*; and the thought of God is *Brahman*. Everything is eternal Soul or *Brahman*.

Krishna says that some people make sacrifices to the gods (angels), some offer their senses in the form of self-control, and others offer their actions in the form of self-control. Some people offer money, some practice austerities, some practice *yoga* (union of all aspects of mind and body). Others study scripture as sacrifice of mundane thoughts, feelings and actions. Some offer breath control (*pranayama*). Some renounce unhealthy foods. Some people help others (*seva*).

Many are the ways to grow on one's spiritual path. All are forms of action that lead to liberation—but inaction alone can never bring liberation. Do not mistake inaction in life as a spiritual attainment. Rather see those who are constantly engaged in trying to improve their lives, the lives of others, helping the environment, and the animals as performing actions leading to spiritual liberation. [Verse 24–32]

Brahma (eternal Soul) is the offering, Brahma is that offered (oblation), Brahma is the sacrificial fire, and Brahma performs the offering. So, by performing actions with this awareness, a person realizes Brahma. [24]

Some yogis propitiate the gods; others make offerings into the fire of Brahma by offering their personal self to the eternal Soul. [25]

Some offer their senses of hearing and seeing into the fire of self-control; others offer sound and other sense objects into the fire of the senses. [26]

Others offer all actions of the senses and their vital energies in the fire of self-control, kindled by wisdom. [27]

Some offer wealth as their sacrifice; some offer austerity and yoga; still others offer study of the scriptures and wisdom. All follow strict vows and self-control. [28]

> *Still others offer their outgoing breath to the incoming breath and vice versa, to achieve cessation of breath; they constantly practice Pranayama. Others regulate their food habits, offering the senses into the breath. [29]*
>
> *All these people know the various forms of sacrifice (offerings). Performing the offerings burns off their impurities. Partaking of the remnants (prashad) they realize their eternal Soul. [30]*
>
> *O Arjuna, one who doesn't perform selfless actions is not fit for this world, what to say about the heavenly realm. [31]*
>
> *There are various offerings prescribed in the Vedas. Understand that they all arise from actions; by knowing this you will become free. [32]*

The Best Ministry

A common question these days is to ask which form of help is the most useful. Some say it is political, social, or ecological activism, helping the poor, the minorities, the environment, etc. Others say it is meditation, since a person must know his or her true self before they can help another person. Still others say that financial donations are the most important.

In the *Bhagavad Gita,* Lord Krishna says that acting with wisdom is superior to uninformed action—even if well-meaning. One such example is donating to a charity without knowledge of how they are spending your money. Some charities give more of the money to the needy while others spend more on administrative fees and fund raising. Knowledge of which charity gives more of your donation to the intended cause makes your donation more beneficial.

Another example is gaining the knowledge of which charities are helping people actually rise out of poverty compared with those who keep throwing money at the situation without changing it. It is important to ensure that your time or money are truly helping.

How to Gain Knowledge

A saint once said that *a true seeker learns something from everyone and everything*. To learn from others requires a person to be humble and sincere and always asking questions to get to the root-cause of situations. This can involve hearing all sides of a situation before coming to a decision; perhaps both sides have good points that need to be integrated into a more holistically helpful answer.

This method of learning equally applies whether learning in school, from a boss or mentor, or from a spiritual guide. Once the root cause of a situation is known; once the false preconceptions and myths are destroyed, one can move forward to affect positive change, without ever becoming confused again.

In the *Bhagavad Gita*, Arjuna is confused about the reasons for fighting this war. Even today, we ask the same questions when countries go to war; why are we fighting? What is the cause of the conflict? Is there any other way than war to settle this?

Dispelling the Myths of Habits of the Poor —the War on Poverty

Here is a modern-day example of finding the root-cause of issues. In the war on poverty, there are many views of the actual cause. Some say the poor were left behind. Others say the wealthy stole and enslaved the poor to become rich themselves. There have also been countless policies to help the poor, most notably those by the International Monetary Fund and the World Bank. But after decades of unsuccessful efforts, people began to analyze and strongly question the effectiveness of these policies.

It took an economics professor from Bangladesh to admit that economic policy as he taught in university could never help the poor. So he directly questioned a group of poor people who earned less than .50 cents (USD) a day. By going to the root of the issue and finding out what was causing the cycle of poverty, he saw past the myth and tried a new approach.

He found that the poor couldn't borrow even tiny amounts of money to purchase the raw goods to make their finished products and sell for a fair price in the market (eg, baskets or unhusked rice). So by giving them small loans for the raw materials, he gave them the opportunity to earn a fair wage.

In running this experiment, many myths were debunked. The poor people were not poor because they were lazy; they just were not given an opportunity. They were not ignorant of running a business; they were not given the opportunity. They were not dishonest; 99% of them repaid their loans. In the end, this professor created a new bank that loaned money only to the poor. And as of 2007, micro-credit or micro-lending banks sprouted around the world and have helped more than 300 million people help themselves out of poverty. They now have a goal, along with the United Nations, to eliminate half the world's poverty by 2015.

So, we see in this example a real act of selfless service—one that applies wisdom, looks beyond the myth, and addresses the root of an issue to truly help make a positive change in the lives of others. This is worthwhile charity work, and one wise way to win a war on poverty.

Finding Solutions Through Alternative Ideas

Once the true reasons for an existing problem are seen clearly, a person can then seek out alternative solutions that will truly help the situation. Just as seeing past the myth that economic theory proffered, seeing that these theories will not help has allowed the professor to seek out the actual dynamics that resulted in abject poverty.

In all aspects of society, including business, health, and education, questioning and seeking the truth beyond the myth, allows a person to discover helpful alternative solutions. But one must be able to think for themselves. For example, in the field of health, there is a general notion in allopathic medicine that disease is addressed by treating symptoms. It is further stated that some diseases cannot be healed and that the causes of some diseases are unknown. Ayurvedic medicine, on the other hand, looks beyond these myths and address-es the root cause of illness, thus these alternative healing methods help many people with so-called incurable disorders.

It is often asked, 'what makes a good leader?' Lately, some have begun to question the view of the 'few knows best' model (few rul-ing the many) because leaders have failed to offer real solutions in many areas of life, such as government, business, education, health, and environment. As people looked past the myth of authoritarian-ism, they found that many successful leaders are listeners; they are servants to their employees and customers; they are compassion-ate, honoring workers rights and environmental health. They fol-low what is called a 'win-win' philosophy. Instead of addressing the outer symptoms of life, they listen to learn the real root-causes of any situation.

If an old-school leader observes that a worker is slowing down, they might use fear or intimidation to 'motivate' that worker. This may work for a short time, but the underlying cause of the slowdown re-mains unaddressed, and unless the situation is resolved, the worker will likely find themselves slowing down again.

Conversely, a leader who seeks out the root of the worker's slowed productivity might ask the worker if everything is alright at home, or if there are any issues at work causing the person to naturally slow down. Studies have found that simply showing more concern about a worker is enough to improve the productivity and job sat-isfaction. Now in the 21st century, most of societies' systems are broken and have not been able to be fixed using the theories of the 20th century. It will require piercing the theoretical myths, seeing the real reason things are broken, and only then will new, successful solutions appear.

Myth-dispelling is at the core of spiritual life as well. Dispelling the myth that the body, feelings, and thoughts are the true Self, is achieved through asking questions such as, 'Who am I' or 'How can I feel God's eternal Divine love'?

The Vedic literature speaks of piercing the veils of illusion (*maya*), the myths of what is real in a temporary sense, compared with what is eternal, and gradually realize one's eternal Soul or eternal bliss (*sat chit ananda*).

Self-Realization means not becoming lost or confused about who you are and what you life purpose is. One sees the eternal in everything—seeing all things as one, undifferentiated. There is no difference between your individual Soul, the Soul of the rock, and God, the Universal Soul, the all-is-One Eternal Soul.

In all areas of life, proper educational methods (ie, direct experience) must be employed to arrive at the root of an issue. This requires continually asking with sincerity and humility.

Krishna says that even the most sinful of sinners can cross the ocean of sin by the boat of knowledge. Here, knowledge means direct experience of Soul or God, and sin means denying oneself the grace of Soul-Realization. We see this in the story of Tulsidass, who was a criminal, but because of his association with saints, he eventually became a saint and wrote *Ramacharita Manasa*, a devotional version of the *Ramayana*.

Some say we are born with 'original sin' and have to work to remove it. It could be argued that if God is within us we are born with 'original grace,' with which we can focus and nurture and grow this Divine aspect of ourselves until it flowers and takes over the rest of our life—no matter how many faults and shortcomings we may have.

The dictionary defines sin as a "transgression of divine law, an estrangement from God." If we follow the laws, our lives flow along with all of nature. So by not sinning one is not restrained from joy, rather, it gives an opportunity to experience the eternal joy inherent in life. While Western religions may teach the above definitions, colloquially, sin is often thought of as an arbitrary offence devised by a vindictive God.

Conversely, the Vedic view is that acting sinfully inflicts self-harm, or at least prevents true joy; destroying one's real dreams and deepest heart's desire. The Vedic standpoint is that one can know God directly, and experience eternal joy even in this life. So the sin of estrangement from God means you are missing an opportunity to experience greater divine joy. It's a shame, not an imposition. In the West sin is something people often want; in the East, sin is something people really want to avoid.

Plant Seeds of Love

Make life a mantra for God—a song of loving praise. Read scriptures, ethical philosophers, spend time in nature and with God's creatures, practice compassion, understanding, and trust; devote all thoughts and actions to God and to the betterment of humans and nature. Share your divine love whenever and wherever you can. Trust others and you will find that most people are trustworthy. In these ways you are constantly planting seeds of love, compassion, and spirit. And we know that nature gives thousands of flowers from just one seed. So by planting God-seeds, you will find your life garden blossoming with God's grace and love.

Giving away the flowers from this garden leaves space for more flowers to grow. And just like some flowers, when it is pruned, two growths appear where there was just one. So the more you give away your Divine love, the more it grows in your life. Once a person tastes the nectar of Divine love—even a drop—they will devote more and more of their actions and thoughts to sharing that nectar, that Divine love.

Wisdom Versus Ignorance

Krishna continues to extol knowledge. He says,
Wisdom is like a fire that reduces all ignorance to ashes. There is nothing as purifying as knowledge. Having faith in something greater than oneself (God, nature, ethics), a person gains greater knowledge. Knowledge in this discussion refers to that gained through experience—not just abstract theory. It is the direct knowledge born of questioning, analyzing, and living that unlocks truth.

A person who doubts their Divine experiences, on the other hand, one who doubts compassion and mistrusts people, cannot know truth. They are lost and cannot find happiness in this world, or in the next world.

The cause of doubt is ignorance. By not questioning, by not searching for the root-cause of issues in life, a person remains only with theories and 'group-think.' If a person does not think for themselves, they can never know truth and remove doubt.

Krishna continues. This form of knowledge is a sword that destroys ignorance and doubt. Thus, it is important to know truth through proper study and to use that knowledge to destroy ignorance and help fix the problems of the world. [Verse 33–42]

O Arjuna, sacrifice of knowledge is superior to sacrifice of material possessions. Actions do not ensnare when performed with wisdom. [33]

This wisdom is learned through reverence, inquiry, and humble service to the wise who have realized their eternal Souls; they will teach you this supreme wisdom. [34]

O Arjuna, by knowing this mystical science you shall never again be deluded; you will realize all creation is in the Soul, and then in Me. [35]

Even the most sinful of the sinners can cross over the ocean of sins and miseries by the bark of this eternal wisdom. [36]

O Arjuna, just as a fire reduces wood to ashes, so too the fire of knowledge burns away (desires for the rewards of) actions. [37]

Nothing in this world purifies like eternal Soul wisdom. Those perfected by yoga, in time, realize this wisdom within themselves. [38]

A person with unflinching faith, who has mastered the senses, realizes their Soul, and thus eternal peace and bliss. [39]

Those ignorant of this teaching are without faith, and this leads to doubt that causes their ruin. For one afflicted by doubt and uncertainty, there is no happiness in this world or the next. [40]

O Arjuna, actions cannot ensnare the person who acts selflessly, self-possessed and uprooting doubt, they realize their eternal, joyful Soul. [41]

Therefore with the sword of eternal knowledge, cut asunder self-doubt born of ignorance that resides in the heart. Take shelter in the mystical science of Self-Realization and arise for battle, O Arjuna. [42]

Summary

Avatars:

- God comes to earth in human form when virtue runs the risk of being destroyed by vice.

- Reincarnation is defined as the Soul moving from body to body until one body realizes they are the Soul. Death is just the exchange of bodies, such as discarding old, worn clothes for new apparel.

- Each religion claims that their God is the only way. There are, in fact, many paths to the same, one goal—Divine realization.

- God created the *gunas* that do the work of creation, maintenance, and destruction in all of life; As eternal and unbounded, God is beyond all activity and material limitations.

Dispelling the Myth of the Caste System:

- People perform best according to their innate God-given abilities, thus making specialization of labor important; one job is not superior to another; all are interdependent.

- Righteous action is action that is done for selfless reasons, and unrighteous actions are those actions that are done for selfish reasons. When a person is aware of their eternally still Soul, even while they are acting, they have succeeded in becoming detached.

Detachment, Gratitude, and Contentment:

- The secrets to easy living: gratitude, contentment, and detachment are discovered when being content with whatever comes without undue effort.

Different Forms of Sacrifice (Selfless Service):

- Sacrifice can involve controlling one's senses, offering money, charity work, austerities, spiritual practices, scriptural study, breath control, and the highest, letting go of personal desires.

How to Gain Knowledge:

- Through sincerity and humility a person gains true knowledge.

Dispelling the Myths of the Habits of the Poor:

- When given an opportunity—a hand-up, the poor prove to be as honest or more honest, reliable, and intelligent as others who have had more opportunities in their life.

Knowledge Through Alternatives:

- Focusing on the root of problems instead of addressing the symptoms, allows you to realize alternative ways to correct situations in all areas of life.

Exercise: Finding the Root of a Problem

- This exercise is to train your thinking to look beyond mere short-term solutions to long-term resolutions. Here you can examine issues in your personal or professional life; review the solutions you have previously tried, and where they have not been successful, review the cause of the problem and see if the earlier solution addressed the cause or just the symptom with a short-term benefit. For example, if you have heartburn and you took an antacid tablet, it gives short-term relief. But if the heartburn returns, then you need to see if you are eating spicy-hot foods, and then try reducing or avoiding them to see if the heartburn disappears. Once the root cause of a situation is discovered, a successful solution will appear. This exercise develops critical thinking and successful problem solving useful for individuals and leaders.

Many paths - One goal

Chapter 5
How to Attain Peace
Through Desireless Action

Arjuna seeks clarification of what appears to be a contradiction. Krishna both renounces action and then recommends performing action. [Verse 1]

> Arjuna said:
> O Krishna, you praise both renunciation of action and performing of action. Between the two, which is better? [1]

Krishna says,
Both paths lead to Self-Realization, but of the two, action is superior. It is difficult to refrain from action (eg, to sit and meditate 20 hours a day), so it is easier to act (ie, action devoted to God and God's children in need). [Verse 2]

> Lord Krishna said:
> Both renunciation of actions and doing prescribed actions lead to liberation. But of the two, fulfilling your responsibilities is superior to renunciation of action. [2]

The person who is constantly engaged in renouncing actions (working for God and God's children), who is self-sufficient (ie, not in the 'give-me' mode), who acts without desire to have or aversion from what comes automatically (eg, pleasure or pain, win and loss, happiness and sorrow) is following the superior path. A person who follows this path is said to be a mental *sannyas* (one who lives for the welfare of others).

This active path allows for a transparent life—one in which the results can be seen. There can be no pretending on this path. Here, action speaks louder than words. Whereas on the path of renunciation, one can say that they have been inactive, but who is there to verify it?

Now Krishna makes a more interesting point:
Renouncing action (*sannyas* or *jnyan yoga*) and acting for others (*karma yoga*) are in fact part of the same *yoga* or two sides of the same coin. Someone who successfully renounces life can gain inner wisdom or Self-Realization; and the successful *karma yogi* (actor) finds wisdom by giving loving action. Both gradually come to realize they are the Divine eternal love.

Those who dedicate their lives to God and helping God's children are free from suffering because suffering arises from personal desire. They are also free from any bondage to virtue, since they are not crediting themselves as the doers of virtuous actions, which would inflate the ego. Both suffering and virtue are binding to the ego. Those who give all credit to God are free from longing and ownership. If all things are the Self, then what is not the Self? There is nothing but Self. Thus, there can be no desire or aversion or the sight of something other than eternal, omnipresent Self. So this person acts only for Self-Realization and helping creation, and not for fame or fortune, and brings about peace.

It is a fair question to ask, how does one develop such a seemingly exalted or rarefied experience? How does one go from self-interest to desiring for Self development and helping God's children?

There are several ways to cultivate selfless actions and thoughts. Parenting requires putting the needs of others first. Parents often go without sleep to tend to a newborn child. They work to earn for their children and for their children's education, health, and happiness. Teaching also requires putting others first. Teachers, like parents, teach children to think of others first. They teach them to be ethical, virtuous, honest, compassionate people and citizens of the community and the world.

Working for or conducting business with socially responsible companies is yet another way to achieve these goals. Companies can exact a fair fee from others for their products and services; they can produce or use renewable energy products; they can also ensure the health and welfare of their workers and their families, including their retirement benefits, and make contributions to the community.

If you review your own lives, you might realize that your basic necessities have always been met. This may inspire you to increase your faith in God or nature or spirit, the provider of basic needs, and live yet more selflessly. Why would God stop providing for you when you are using your God-given gifts to help others? Thus, your minds are freed to spend more of your time sharing your innate gifts and helping others.

Focusing on God and Helping Others

Here are some personal, family, business, and social examples of how to focus on God and helping others, already built into our cultural lifestyles. Spiritually, the process is a matter of letting go of the ownership of your actions, the senses, and your ego, as you become more aware of your inner God-given gifts—the things you 'love' to do, and the things that are second nature for you. As you realize these gifts, develop and share them with others in need (outside of yourselves and your own individual needs). This cultivates spiritual progress. They are a form of *sadhana* (meditation): *bhakti-karma yoga* (service-oriented action).

Silent *sadhana* (seated with eyes closed) is another important way to know the Self as eternal Divine love (*sat chit ananda*). Reading scriptures and having spiritual conversations (*satsang*) and singing songs to God (*bhajans*) are other important forms of *sadhana* that cultivate a whole, spiritual person. Seeing the sacred in all acts (eg, cooking, cleaning) are also forms of *sadhana*.

Verse 13 provides a unique insight. For those who live with the guilt that they somehow caused another's hardships (eg, 'I caused my parents divorce' or 'If I had been more alert, I could have prevented the disaster'), this verse shows how the nonmoving Soul can neither take credit nor blame for events in the world. Of course, this notion can be misused by those who abnegate their personal responsibilities in life; but that is not the intent of these verses. [Verse 3–13]

Know that the person who has neither longing nor desire for rewards of action is ever renouncing (sannyas); O mighty-armed, that person is free from all dualities and is easily liberated from bondage. [3]

In truth, the wise know that renunciation of action and performing righteous action is the same thing; those of unclear thinking believe otherwise. A person fully following one path receives the rewards of both. [4]

The state realized by renunciants is also envisioned by those acting dutifully. Those who see wisdom and responsible action as the same are true seers. [5]

O mighty-armed, it is difficult to achieve renunciation of action without performing action. The wise, devoted to action, quickly realize their eternal nature. [6]

The person devotedly fulfilling their obligations (yoga) are purified mentally, self-subjugated, and master of their senses; they realize their inner eternal Soul as the same universal eternal Soul in all beings; their selfless actions do not subjugate them. [7]

The self-aware, knower of Truth realizes they are not the doer, rather it is the senses that see, hear, touch, smell, eat, walk, breathe, speak, grasp, release, and blink the eyes (involuntary actions). This person realizes it is the senses alone that are active (not their eternal Soul). [8, 9]

Those who perform selfless action, surrendering all work to Brahman (eternal Soul), sin does not attach to them, like water on a lotus leaf. [10]

For the reason of self-purification alone, karma yogis (righteous actors) act with their body, mind, intellect, and senses, without desire for reward. [11]

Those steady-minded people who carry out dutiful action without desire for rewards realize uninterrupted peace. The unsteady-minded, having a desire for rewards, becomes enslaved by their obsession. [12]

The steady-minded, through renouncing self-centered desires through mental discrimination, realize they are not the doer of action, nor cause others to act; and so live happily in the city of the 9 gates (body). [13]

You Can be Happy or You Can be Right

Personal interactions between oneself and other persons can teach one how to let go of ownership and how to serve others. It is easy to find fault in others, seeing their mistakes and judging what is right or wrong, calling them lazy, thoughtless, or careless; rude, or inconsiderate. But who are we to judge anyone else? It is most likely they are doing their best, and who says we do not come across the same way to others? Moreover, who are we to decide what is the 'right way', or know for certain why things occur? Can anyone really know the cause and effect of *karma*—actions completed in past lives? Humans tend to seek reasons for why things happen. In reality, however, we have little understanding of the cause and effect of our actions or the actions of others or of circumstances around us. Why did the weather turn cold, why did the stock market go up? There are many factors, that we cannot begin to grasp the truth of the matter.

This explanation should not be used as an excuse to run rampant. There are rules and laws within societies to be followed. Conversely, if someone has views different from your own, rather than seeing the differences, see their Soul.

It is a fickle mind—attached and desiring fame, fortune, material things—that seeks to be 'right.' That mind is ever bound by action. Fighting to be 'right' keeps one's mind and heart in a state of criticism and battle. So one simple way to attain peace is to let go of having to be right. Have a steady mind and be happy. Here are some examples contrasting a fickle and a steady mind.

Fickle Mind	Steady Mind
Live to eat	Eat to live
Keep up with the Joneses (buying whatever new things neighbors are buying)	Whatever material things you have—be content; share what you have to help others less fortunate.
Desire to be recognized	Desire to serve well
Desire to be 'right'	Desire to feel content
Quid pro quo: I'll help you if you help me	Allowing helping to be its own reward

[Verse 14–17]

> *God does not create the body, the actions of the world, or the results of action; it is nature that is responsible for all action. [14]*
>
> *The omnipresent God is not involved with the virtues or vices of anyone. Wisdom is hidden by ignorance, so people are deluded. [15]*
>
> *But for those who have vanquished their ignorance through knowing their Self, this Soul awareness is like the Sun, illuminating the Eternal Self. [16]*
>
> *Those whose wisdom has shaken off the ignorance, realizing spiritual intelligence, who meditate on the inner eternal Self, who has perfected faith (based on experience), and who have taken refuge in the Lord, attain spiritual freedom (from mundane entrapments). [17]*

The Steady Mind

Next Krishna discusses the even-minded state of a wise person. He cites as an example that, the wisest people see all of life with an equal eye—from the holiest and wisest person to the vilest creature. They see the Soul in each person.

This point is often misinterpreted. Some may say, well, if all is the same (Soul), nothing matters, so I won't do anything. I won't care for my physical self or others. This interpretation is incorrect and is used to justify lazy, uncaring behavior. It is a great shame to waste one's God-given gifts by becoming inactive, by not enjoying your gifts, by not trying to make this a better world. Remember, Krishna told Arjuna to act and lovingly help others.

If a person feels they are above having to act for another because he or she has achieved total realization of Oneness, ask them then to demonstrate that they have attained an exalted state beyond mere intellectual understanding. Ask them to walk through the wall to show that they and the wall are one. If they can not, they do not truly understand the Oneness through experience.

This is why Krishna said earlier,
Even God acts or the entire universe will cease to exist.

So when we speak of all as one, keep in mind the context in which it is stated. Try to see the sacred thread of God or spirit in all things.

This promotes respect, worship, contentment, and bliss; quite the opposite from the sloth of inaction.

Thus, Krishna says,
Treat all things and people—the highest and lowest—with equal respect for their inner sacredness.

As the Vedic principle states, *charity begins at home*. So make sure you are following a healthy lifestyle and Ayurvedic food plan; see that your family is also following the same. Ensure that the basic needs of the family are covered in the present and for the future (eg, plan and save for your children's college education). Then look to the extended family, and next look to the neighbors. Check to see if anyone needs help. In this way, help gradually expands outward beyond the immediate family. It is said that helping a large cause and ignoring local needs is a form of pride; 'look at me, I help this well-known cause'.

Another maxim admonishes that we serve guests first. We should serve guests as if God has come to our home. So we are advised to feed them before we feed our own family; see to their comfort before we can feel comfortable. So in our immediate environment, first serve those who visit, then our families, then when all is cared for at home, serve the extended community.

Thus, the wise are content with all that comes their way—neither desiring for good or happiness or money; nor do they recoil or grieve from hearing bad or unpleasant news. Since all happiness and sadness are temporal, the one who can experience the eternal Soul cannot be unbalanced by good or bad news. With the mind focused on eternal contentment that is God, and serving God's children, temporal issues become less important.

There is a story about a Native American Indian tribe that illustrates this thought. The chief called all the young boys to teach them to be warriors, but one boy was not chosen because he was il. The people told the boy's father that this was bad news indeed.

The father only said, 'perhaps.'

The boy wandered out on his own one day and found a wild horse. He brought it back to the chief. The people told the boy's father that this was good news indeed.

The father only said, 'perhaps.'

After a few days the horse ran away. The people told the boy's father that this was bad news indeed.

The father only said, 'perhaps.'

The horse told the other wild horses how well he was treated by the people that they all came back to the tribe with the first horse. The chief was so pleased he gifted the boy with a horse.

The people told the boy's father that this was good news indeed.

The father only said, 'perhaps.'

As the boy was riding the horse he fell off and broke his leg.

The people told the boy's father that this was bad news indeed.

The father only said, 'perhaps.'

The chief led a war party and many of the boys were killed. But because the father's boy was home with a broken leg, his life was saved. The people told the boy's father that this was good news indeed.

The father only said, 'perhaps.'

So we can never know what is good or bad for us. What appears to be bad or challenging for us one day, might turn out to strengthen our integrity and develop our wisdom down the road. When life is too easy, one becomes spoiled and begins to feel entitled and ungrateful for the God-given gifts they have received.

Contentment Versus Emotionlessness

In discussions on the state of contentment (a balanced life, being neither happy nor sad), a point is sometimes raised: if a person lives beyond happiness and sadness, would that not make them as emotionless as a robot? Well then, if one is not balanced, would they not become victims of their emotions? The reality is that being beyond emotions means that one's Soul or consciousness is awake to its own eternal, nonchanging existence. So while happiness and sadness cycle through life, one is inside their eternal experience and is not knocked off course by emotional events. Just as during a rainstorm, if you are inside the house, you are less affected by the weather.

Moreover, those who are more aware of their eternal Soul have a greater ability to feel whatever emotion a life event brings, because they are not afraid of being swallowed up by these emotions. They can remain open and balanced and are able to make the wisest decisions even during hectic and emotional times. They will be less likely let situations overtake them. A clear-minded person chooses what is best for their life-purpose—that is, what is best for all people and nature—when they remain in harmony with that nature. A person who is enslaved by their emotions, in times of extremes, makes decisions based on personal, short-term needs. So it is not that a person is emotionless. Rather, they are able to feel the full range and depth of emotions without being overcome by them. In this way, they can continue to serve others in the best way possible—free from being overwrought by circumstances.

The Enlightened Person

Lord Krishna notes that the Enlightened person, the one who sees all things as eternal Soul, helps all beings. Such a person can see the grace in others—their Godlike qualities—and serves all people equally. There is no judgment, no helping only 'good' people and ignoring 'bad' or 'evil' people. They do their best to serve all people who cross their paths. And in doing so, they attain full liberation.

Again, the reader is cautioned to not take this statement as an absolute. Each person has a range of influence: there are some people you can help and others you cannot. For example, in the Ayurvedic health system, it advises the practitioner to help those they can help, and honestly admit when they cannot help someone.

It is good for readers to reflect on their own lives to see how open their hearts are to their own loved ones, co-workers, and neighbors. In this way, you can see if you treat people equally without judgment or malice.

When loneliness, loss, grief, and emptiness do not break one's spirit; when anger and lust no longer control a person; when happiness, fame, and good fortune are not a cause for becoming drunk with happiness to the point of ignoring responsibilities; when even sadness can be welcomed with feelings of gratefulness; when everyone and everything is seen as the God-spirit—the *sat chit ananda* or eternal bliss of spirit or God or nature, only then can one be said to be fully liberated from material life.

Another way to describe this experience is that when a person feels there is nothing to gain or lose in life—that where one is now is fine to be, and that contentment or peace can be realized regardless of one's circumstances, this is a form of liberation, that is, freedom from external negative or limited influence.

In reality, it is impossible to describe the state of *sat chit ananda*. As Lord Krishna says, it is not really outward appearances that determine internal realization. Even the great Indian saint Ramakrishna, when he was informed a spiritual council determined that he was Self-Realized, said that he didn't know what the term meant; that he was the same person now as he was before receiving the news: nothing had changed, so the 'outer' words meant nothing to him.

The understanding of Self-Realization is often confused by people's projections of what they believe such enlightened behavior would be like; however, in reality, each enlightened person has a very unique personality and life experience. At the end of his life, the saint Paramahamsa Yogananda said that in his next life, he will be not be a leader, but instead be the person sitting in the back of the room that no one notices.

Nowadays, much more is made of the notion of Self-Realization than is merited. There is a saying:

> *Before enlightenment, chop wood and carry water.*
> *After enlightenment, chop wood and carry water.*

The external person is the same. The enlightened person behaves normally, not calling attention to himself or herself. *Bhaktas* (people who feel great love and devotion toward God), do not even ask for *moksha* (Self-Realization), because it would mean sacrificing the feeling of loving God and knowing that God love's them. Although the issue of *moksha* sells books and spiritual courses, apart from the commercial arena, it is a term that more often than not, keeps the intellect engaged in some personal illusion of what *moksha* is or would be like, while preventing the growth of experiencing the grace of devotion in the living present.

> *Trust no future, no matter how pleasant.*
> *Let the dead past bury its dead.*
> *Act, act in the living present.*
> *Heart within and God overhead*

So instead of divorcing Self-Realization from compassion, remember that the aim of *moksha* is to end suffering. How each person grows in peace and compassion will differ, because every path to God is unique.

It is impossible to describe the state of *moksha*, since it is beyond words. So what is written here is merely a feeble attempt to illuminate and should not be taken as an absolute. The only absolute is the eternal Soul.

As this wisdom, based in experience, grows stronger, peace becomes stronger, and the less the mind, emotions, senses, and desires battle for attention. This is called mental *sannyas*, or keeping a strong, detached, compassionate mind in the midst of an active life. Some major pointers to developing such an exalted state include:

1. Acknowledge abundance in your life

2. Follow a healthy lifestyle and Ayurvedic food plan

3. Discover and follow your life-purpose (*dharma*) and work toward short- and long-term visions.

4. Do good for others or at least do not cause harm

5. Do not run after fame and fortune

6. Read the scriptures and other uplifting compassionate writings

7. Credit all actions and results thereof to God or nature or spirit

8. Use intuition and common sense   [Verse 18–29]

Only those who see a holy person endowed with wisdom and humility, a cow, an elephant, a dog and a pariah with equal vision have realized genuine wisdom. [18]

Those who have equanimity of mind conquer this world in this lifetime, because they are endowed with an equality of vision of the eternal, and are free from all dualities of life; they are established in God awareness. [19]

Completely rooted in eternal awareness and understanding eternal Self, self-possessed of spiritual wisdom, undeluded, neither rejoicing nor grieving upon receiving pleasant or unpleasant life events. [20]

One whose Self is not attached to the external sense objects enjoys the inner delight of Self. God-realized through union of small and cosmic Self, they enjoy eternal bliss. [21]

Pleasures from sense objects are a source of misery as they have a beginning and an end. O Arjuna, this is why the spiritually wise never seek delight in them. [22]

The person who is not ruled by physical and emotional desires in their life is self-controlled and truly happy. [23]

Those who have found inner eternal joy, pleasure, and light, have become established in God-love realization—eternal freedom. [24]

The knowers of Truth (rishis) whose doubts have been dispelled, whose sins have been cleansed, act only to help all beings; they realize eternal liberation. [25]

Those who have renounced (temporal material pleasures), are free from lust and anger, and are Self-Realized; they experience absolute freedom now and forever. [26]

Those whose mind ignores external sense-objects, with eyes fixed between the eyebrows, and stilled in and out breaths inside the nostrils, that person has controlled their senses, mind and spiritual intelligence. Free from desire, fear and anger, they are fully focused on Soul liberation as their supreme goal, they are liberated forever. [27-28]

Knowing Me to be the receiver and dispenser of offerings (yajna) and austerity, the Supreme Lord of the Universe, and the friend of all beings, they realize eternal peace. [29]

Summary

• By not holding onto material possessions or seeking fame, fortune, and power, and instead crediting all to God and by cultivating a sense of gratitude and grace, and being non-judgmental, individuals can undergo the renunciation of worldly things and feel a greater sense of intimate love between themselves and God.

Exercise: Let Go-Give Credit

This exercise has three parts to it.

1. Honestly review your actions, words, and thoughts about a situation that is causing undue stress or discomfort in your personal or professional life. Do you see where you may be trying to hold on, for recognition, or being right? [Please don't judge yourself over this, for that will only impede your achieving peace and contentment and resolution of this issue.]

2. Once you see where your personal desires are involved, review the successes that led you to this desire, and credit God for giving you such God-gifts (eg, memory, courage, adaptability, leadership, communication skills). Try to see that while you were successful, whose powers, whose gifts were they that allowed you to be successful. If you can honestly see these innate abilities are God-gifts, you can then thank God for your success, and be grateful that you were able to help improve a situation. Since God has given you the success, you can relax and accept that God has also given the outcome. So if you didn't get as much recognition, financial or status remuneration, remember that the spiritual suggestion is to do your best to help—just for the sake of helping. Virtue is its own reward. You can see that you did not lose by doing your best. Become aware of the feelings arising from you being the one chosen to help. Once you stop defining the lack of fame, fortune, or power that didn't come to you as unfair or punishment, and note that, in an idealistic way, that you were able to be involved in a helping project, you

should see how good you feel inside. [If you truly feel you were taken advantage of, then you need to address that as a separate issue.]

3. Once you can let go, you are able to thank God for such a feeling. As you feel more gratitude for each outcome you will find life more meaningful, and you will find more opportunities come your way since you appreciate all that God has given you to this point. Moreover, since you enjoy helping others, you will find more opportunities to be of greater help to more people over time. Help can mean physically, monetarily, through sharing ideas (eg, writing, lecturing), etc. All the time you can check and see that you're basic needs in life are provided for (ie, you are not neglecting your responsibilities to earn a living and provide for your family, get good grades in school, or being taken advantage of).

For some people, letting go may mean allowing yourself to slow down and enjoy life more; appreciating family, friends, and nature. Finding the cause of the stress lies in questioning the basic premise that you use to view a situation (eg, 'I cannot relax'). If you can see that you deserve to relax, the stress will resolve itself immediately.

Mohandas Gandhi; father of the modern-day social responsibility (eg, fair trade, micro-lending, environmental concerns, non-violent protest). Martin Luther King said Gandhi's teachings inspired his own nonviolent movement in the USA.

Chapter 6
How to Attain Peace
Through Selfless Service

Lord Krishna explains that a *sannyasi* or *yogi* (one who acts from within their core, directly experiencing the individual and universal Soul) is one who lives responsibly, without seeking rewards for his or her work. Achieving this level of realization requires a combination of knowledge and experience—one or the other alone is insufficient. Intellectual ideas are only theory until tested through experience, and experiencing something without intellectual confirmation can cause doubt about the experience.

For a *sannyasi*, doing good is its own reward. In modern day life, there are many examples of selfless action: not polluting the earth, air, or water; helping the less fortunate, while not seeking recognition or financial gain for your help.

A recent trend is finding some corporations rewriting their bylaws to reflect their commitment to selfless service. Their mission statement shows a triple accountability to people, the planet, and to profit. Inspired by Gandhi's social movement these visionary corporations are taking peaceful resistance to the next level and creating better opportunities for their workers or giving large sums of money for civic or humanitarian purposes. This is called *seva* (selflessly serving humanity and nature). Most if not all corporations have always given to charity, but here we are highlighting the redressing of human and environmental responsibility back into corporate bylaws; taking a wider look at corporate humanitarianism. This is an example of 'mental' *sannyas*; people who made the decision to triple-win business vision.

Other examples of mental *sannyas* include many teachers around the world who devote their lives to their work out of love for the children. Often, teachers spend their own hard-earned money on student supplies and work many hours at home to prepare for the next day. These are modern-day examples of helping as its own reward. [Verse 1–4]

Lord Krishna said:

People whose actions are dedicated to God without desire for the rewards of the actions is a true renouncer (sannyas) and one who unites inner and cosmic Self (yogi); not those who do not fulfill their responsibilities nor those who perform no action. [1]

O Arjuna, that which is called renunciation (sannyas) is also known as uniting inner and cosmic Self (yoga). No one can be a yogi without giving up sensory desires. [2]

Action is the means for the muni aiming for Self-Realization. When that person has attained this realization, inaction is then the means. [3]

When a person is not addicted to sensory gratification, action nor the rewards of actions, they are said to have attained Self-Realization. [4]

Service versus Sadism

When a person acts to help others without personal reward, there are often many rewards: peace, wealth, and bliss. Some might ask, 'if I choose to not look out for my personal needs, what if I wind up deceived, alone, and penniless? Only deceit yields deceit (as you sow, so shall you reap/*karma*). Moreover, if a person is sincerely helping God's children, why would God punish that person for such work?

We see this question in business, politics, organizations, and in many individuals. 'We can't change this policy to help reduce pollution—it will make our business lose money.' 'I can't take time to help a person now because I have so many responsibilities.' 'I can't fight for the passage of this bill because too many people would vote me out of office.' Yet, in each case, once the change was implemented, everyone benefited. In some cases a person may lose their job, but what is a job worth if it is not helping people and one's conscience cannot live with themselves? Look to the next career that person lands, and then see if they have more contentment and respect for themselves and their career.

It is important to analyze the notion whether God punishes people for doing things such as preserving nature or protecting or helping people. The punishing viewpoint suggests a vindictive God. True, life may change for the 'do-gooder'; they may wind up in a new position or place. But this would be because they will be able to help more people and the planet in this new situation, not because God is vindictive or sadistic. A person will only feel the outcome of following their conscience is a punishment when they have a preconceived notion of what is 'supposed' to happen, what is the 'right' way, or look to what other people say. Conversely, choosing the position 'I must always follow my conscience' as the non-changing mark, then the results either immediately reveal a better situation, or in time, reveal a positive outcome or a blessing in disguise.

We see evidence that this philosophy of helping others brings success instead of punishment. Social entrepreneurs, following universal principles, are finding that compassion, ethics, and profit can operate together successfully. Many socially responsible investment company's money market funds are yielding higher profits than their counterparts who continue to employ age-old worker and environmental abuses.

We also see examples of selfless actions in parents who love their children, putting the children's needs first; feeding, clothing, educating, protecting, loving their children without regard for financial reward or fame, or from receiving short-term outbursts of , 'I hate you mommy and daddy.'

Thus, to be unattached to anything, that is, to be unconcerned about the rewards that may come from doing good, describes a selfless, unselfish person—a *yogi* or a mental *sannyasi*. The way to raise oneself up in this manner is through the Soul (*atman*). The more a person is aware of their Soul, the more guidance they will find in life.

A person who acts selflessly does not care about fame or dishonor, wealth or poverty, pleasure or pain. They act in the name of the Soul (the Eternal) and let others say and judge as they will. That person knows who they are and why they act.

Such a person sees God in all people—friend or enemy. This realization is achieved through persistent meditation and by focusing the mind's heart on God. This is called *satsang* or being in the presence of holy people (including God). Gradually, this constant exposure transforms one's body, mind, emotions, intellect, senses, and subtle body in tune with God.

Verses 10-13 offer instructions how to meditate. Yet these ideas are best to be taken as examples rather than the 'only way' to meditate. Meditation is best done in a clean place where you are not disturbed, such as a study or backyard. The idea of 'controlling you mind' is tricky because the word 'control' suggests force. Natural meditation means not straining to find peace as forcing thoughts out causes more stress.

Many people say, "I cannot stop thinking". This is fine. A general suggestion is to just return to your form of meditation when you can. Meditating on God or whatever brings you some peace is beneficial. It is also difficult and unnatural to sit motionless and in perfect posture. For some this works; for others they need to feel comfort and the ability to shift when uncomfortable. Staring at the tip of one's nose is just one example of a meditation style. [Verse 5–16]

The person must raise themselves by their Self. They must not lower themselves. For they are their own friend or enemy to their Self. [5]

For the person who has conquered their mind, their mind is their best friend. But for those with uncontrolled minds, their mind is their worst enemy. [6]

They who have conquered their mind, understanding beyond dualities of cold/heat, happiness/unhappiness, honor/dishonor, are completely rooted in their eternal Soul (paramatma). [7]

Those who are satisfied with wisdom from direct experience of Soul, who have conquered the senses and is even-minded; for those who see a lump of clay, a stone, and gold as the same; that yogi is said to be a saint established in Self-Realization (yukta). [8]

More esteemed still is the sage who treats all people equally, be they friends, well-wishers, enemies, neutrals, mediators, envious, saintly, or unrighteous people. [9]

A yogi consistently remaining alone in a secluded place, controlling their mind, desireless, freed from ownership, should meditate on their inner Soul. [10]

In a sacred and clean spot, fixing a seat that is neither too high nor too low, with kusha grass, deerskin, and natural fabric. [11]

Seated there, fixed minded, subduing the mind and senses, they are to practice yoga (union of individual self and cosmic Self) for purifying their mind—virtuous and honest. [12]

Hold the body, head, and neck erect, motionless, with fixed gaze on the tip of the nose, without looking around in any other direction. [13]

Full of inner peace, fearless, steadfast in the vow of celibacy, controlling the mind; the renunciant, sits absorbed in thoughts of Me, regarding Me as their supreme goal. [14]

Thus, ever engaged in meditation on the Self, the person aiming to unite inner Soul with cosmic Soul (yoga), with mind directed inward, attains eternal peace that exists in Me. [15]

O Arjuna, union of individual and cosmic Selves (yoga) does not occur for those who eat too much or too little, nor for those who sleep too much or too little. [16]

The Middle Path

The actions of such a selflessly serving person are moderate. A great Soul is one who lives a modest, balanced life. This too, was Lord Buddha's message: follow the middle path.

Krishna observes that the practice of this *yoga* path is not for those who work, eat, play, or sleep too much or too little (eg, fasting, all-night vigils). But the person who lives a balanced life, allows for the possibility that all misery can be destroyed.

This is a fantastic and crucially important point, because there have been so many myths surrounding being a *yogi*. The general misconception is that you have to fast or sit in meditation without eating or sleeping, or that you cannot have any fun in life, or that you have to practice severe *tapas* (austerities). But Lord Krishna clearly dispels this misleading and dangerous myth. Moderation is the mantra.

The person who lives in this *yogic* state is said to be like a lamp in a windless spot, that is, one that does not flicker. So too, the *yogi's* mind does not waver. Once achieving this state the person does not fall back to the former life of personal desires (*sannyasi* also means to not return to the past lower life levels). Through a path of moderation, a person is no longer overwhelmed by life's demands or overtaken by emotion because in moderation, things are not allowed to build up unduly. Such a person is more open to experiencing what comes to them in life—whatever it may be.

For those wishing to attain mental peace, it is advised to withdraw the mind from the senses and outer worldly affairs by thinking of the needs of others, and gradually by degrees, releasing themselves from the grip of desires. In this way, they will attain peace. The person who sees God in all things and all things within God is that *yogi/sannyasi*. God never leaves them, and they never leave God. They have realized and attained eternal life with God, in God, even while alive (ie, their Soul realizes its eternal nature). [Verse 17–32]

Moderation of eating, recreation, fulfilling responsibilities (karma), sleep and wakefulness, is able to remove all misery. [17]

When the mind, completely controlled, rests solely in the Self, then without attachment to all material desires, that person is declared united with eternal Soul (yukta). [18]

The yogi who has united individual and cosmic Selves behaves like a flame in a windless place [19]

When the mind, united through the development of yoga, attains serenity, they then perceive the inner Self by the Self; that person is satisfied in the Self alone. [20]

In this state, beyond the senses, the yogi experiences eternal bliss that is experienced due to purified understanding; knowing that and being established in this state, they never lose their Self-Realization. [21]

From realizing this state, the person doesn't consider any other attainment greater that that. Being completely established in this state, the person is never overwhelmed even by intense suffering. [22]

Know that perfection is the union of individual and cosmic Self; it is freedom from miseries due to material contact. [23]

It is one's duty to ever abandon all desires for sensory gratification due to mental thoughts, withdrawing all the senses from all directions. [24]

Through conviction, as one experiences their mind gradually becoming established in the Self, the mind does not think of anything else. [25]

Let the person withdraw their mind wherever the restless and unsteady mind may wander; let them bring the mind under control by the Self alone. [26]

The person who is free from passion, tranquil minded, who has become one with God, freed from all impurities; they experience supreme bliss. [27]

Permanently experiencing the union of the individual and cosmic Self, the yogi is free from all that ensnares, and thus experiences their inner eternal joy of God. [28]

The Self-Realized person (united individual and cosmic Self) experiencing this Self everywhere and in everything, realizes the Self in all creatures and all creatures in the Self. [29]

> *That person who sees Me everywhere and everything in Me, I am never out of their awareness and they are never out of my awareness. [30]*
>
> *For the yogi who knows I reside in the heart of all creatures, offers their devoted service to Me; they remain with me at all times. [31]*
>
> *O Arjuna, a yogi is one who, by comparison to their inner Self, sees the same true Self equally in all creatures, be they in their pleasure and pain. [32]*

Arjuna, his mind still restless, asks Krishna how a person can become permanently peaceful. [Verse 33–34]

> *Arjuna said:*
> *O Krishna, this union of individual and cosmic Self (yoga) by even-mindedness that you described, I do not see its lasting experience due to the restless nature of the mind. [33]*
>
> *O Krishna, the mind is restless, turbulent, strong and obstinate; I feel it is more difficult to subdue than the wind. [34]*

This is a common question people ask today when the topic of meditation is mentioned (eg, 'how can I remain peaceful when the baby needs a 1 a.m. feeding, when I have bills to pay, when the boss yells at me?') Krishna assures him that through persistence, dedication, sincerity of purpose, and dispassionate practice, the mind can become peaceful. It requires self-regulation. [Verse 35–36]

> *Lord Krishna said:*
> *O mighty armed, indeed the mind is restless and difficult to master; but O Arjuna, it can be controlled through practice and detachment from sense gratification. [35]*
>
> *For those with an uncontrolled mind, yoga is difficult to obtain, but controlling the mind is attainable through right means. This is My opinion. [36]*

Arjuna then asks, What happens to the person who, trying to reach this state, cannot attain it in this lifetime? Do they perish? Are they punished? Again, the notion of a vindictive, sadistic God is broached. [Verse 37–39]

> Arjuna said:
> What is the fate of a person of faith, whose mind wanders away from yoga due to lack of self-control? [37]
>
> O Mighty armed, does this confused person, deviating from the path to Self-Realization, without sanctuary, perish like dispersing cloud? [38]
>
> O Krishna, I beseech you to dispel this doubt of mine completely; there is none but you who can remove this doubt. [39]

Krishna confirms that not only will a person not be punished in this world, but also they will not meet with sadness even in the next world. The law of *karma*, the laws of science and even Western religions say that every action has an equal and opposite reaction: as you sow, so shall you reap. So in helping others, you can only rise toward God's grace.

Should a person fall from their good efforts, or die while trying to do good works, they go to a world (heaven) of righteous Souls, and live there for some time until their merit is exhausted, then they are born into families of great integrity and spirituality (eg, a family might be a family of *yogis*), and continue their lives from where they left off in their last life…quickly fulfilling their purpose this time around. [Verse 40–43]

> Lord Krishna said:
> O Arjuna, for anyone engaged in virtuous activity, there is no destruction for them in this life or the next, they never come to an evil end. [40]
>
> The person who falls from the path of yoga, ascends to the heavens; remaining there for a long time, they take rebirth in a pure and prosperous family. [41]
>
> Or they may be born into a family of wise yogis; though this is certainly a very rare occurrence in this world. [42]
>
> O Arjuna, through this cycle, that person now continues with his past-life spiritual development, and strives even more for perfection. [43]

Krishna further clarifies the point by saying,
A sincere inquiry into *yoga*, brings a person beyond the rites and rituals normally required of a person.

If you really want to know God, you do not need a middleman or rules and rituals. When a baby cries, the mother does not say, I won't go to the baby until they address me by my proper name. The mother runs to the baby to see to its needs. So too, when God's children sincerely cry for God, God runs to give them love.

The *yogi* (the performer of service, with even mind, with wisdom based on their experiences) is considered more special than just the person who practices austerities, or rituals, or just has book learning of the subject. For it is that *yogi* who is happy with God and absorbed in God with unflinching faith.

This is why this chapter is entitled *dhyan*—unswerving focus on God. [Verse 44–47]

Due to the merit of their previous practice, they are again irresistibly attracted. Even an inquiry about yoga surpasses the literal principles of the Vedas. [44]

Diligently persevering, purified of worldly attachment, that yogi achieves the perfection of many lifetimes, and attains the Supreme Self-Realization. [45]

That yogi is superior to ascetics who attained only intellectual knowledge; and to those who act for self-reward (sense gratification). Therefore, O Arjuna, be a yogi. [46]

To me, of all the yogis, the highest is the one whose inner self is absorbed in Me with full faith; worshipping Me through devotional service. [47]

Summary

- When a person realizes that their basic needs are met in life, they no longer need to think about or focus on their needs. In turn, they begin to think about others, for example, the needy, those who can use their help. By sharing with others, one can feel their lives become more and more sacred. From this, they develop increasingly more gratitude and also a greater bond with Divine Love. It is this blissful, divine love that keeps God foremost in their minds.

Endnote

Social Awareness in Modern-Day Corporations

Several dot.com companies are donating money to help improve science education. These people hope to see the next generation of children become educationally prepared to take technology to the next level.

Some companies are retooling so their factories not only decrease the amount of pollution they emit but to send out cleaner air and water than they took in for manufacturing. Their products are vegetable-based, so they are not only biodegradable, but they also nourish the soil when they decompose.

Although some corporations are acting responsibly—as the *Bhagavad Gita* admonishes them to do—they are also finding themselves reaping many unforeseen benefits such as increased peace owing to better working relations and realizing higher profits.

Other corporations form social entrepreneurships whose sole mission is to help the impoverished help themselves to a better life and work themselves out of poverty and abuse. Through small, low-interest loans (micro-credit or micro-lending), the poor have the opportunity to work their way out of poverty.

In the process many myths are being shattered. They are finding that the poor are smart enough and have ample will and integrity to run businesses on their own. They are also repaying their loans more quickly than the national average. Such simple aims have resulted in more than 300,000 people coming out of poverty as of 2007, and the Nobel Peace Prize was awarded to the developer of microcredit, Muhammad Yunnus. We see how helping people rise out of poverty has wide-reaching effects—improving the prospects for world peace. So we never know how our good actions will influence others, but clearly, from the above example, its effect will be positive.

Companies are doing good for its own reward and are finding immense satisfaction seeing that many people are no longer poverty stricken.

Exercises:

1. Review your life, examining how your basic needs (food, clothing, and shelter) are met. Have you found that somehow the money appears when you really need it? Do you find you do not need to struggle unduly to get yours or your family's basic needs met?

   Now look to the non-essential things you strive for; maybe a few fancier options on your car, a more expensive clothing brand, or going to some trendy vacation spot? Do you find you have to struggle much harder to earn for these items? Do you find these struggles to be a source of stress, anger, alienation, or impatience? If so, you have isolated the cause of many of your undue stresses.

   How the term 'basic needs' is defined will differ slightly from family to family, so there is no judgement intended in the above example. A couple saving to pay for their child's college education has more basic needs than a couple whose children have graduated college. It is not the intention here to offer one definition of basic needs for all people. Once you define your family's own basic needs you will find it useful to review the exercise from your personal standpoint.

2. If you have found that your basic needs are met without undue struggle, now look to the next step. Review the times that you

have helped others in need without asking for anything in return. Did you receive some special inner feeling? Did you find that while helping your own needs were met with even less focus or effort?

3. Think of times when your actions were dictated by your conscience and not fear of financial or social retribution. Did things ultimately work out for you better than imagined?

Our basic needs are met by God, so we can serve others

Chapter 7
How to Know God

Lord Krishna begins by telling Arjuna how to know the eternal God through the fixed mind and faithful persistence, noting how rare it is to find a person able to achieve God-Realization. God's lower nature (*prakrti*) includes the 5 elements (ether, air, fire, water, and earth), and the mind, intellect, and ego, whereas God's higher nature is eternal Soul (*atma*).

God is the origin of creation and also the one who causes its dissolution. There is nothing and no one higher than God.

Krishna says that like a strand of pearls on a thread, everything and everyone in this creation is as a bead strung on God's necklace. God is in everything and everyone. Moreover, God is the best aspect of each thing: the intellect of the intelligent, the radiance in the moon and sun, and the prowess in the powerful. God is strength devoid of desire and attachment, and also the desire that is not against righteous living (*dharma*).

Because people only see the material world, they are misled by its true essence (God), and thus do not see or know God. The *gunas* create a mysterious veil (*maya*) that prevents people from seeing beyond the mundane and into the eternal nature of God.

Those whose actions are more harmful, wicked, and corrupt do not care to know God, but virtuous-behaving people do. There are four types of virtuous people that worship God:

1. The distressed

2. Seekers of knowledge

3. Seekers of material prosperity

4. Wise servants or worshipers of God

The wise are the most devoted and focused of the four types of worshippers, for they have no other desire but God. It is rare to find such a noble Soul. God is dearest to them and they are dearest to God.

People whose focus is distracted by various desires worship lesser gods through prayers, rites, and rituals in the hope of gaining pleasure, power, fame, fortune, and so on. [Verse 1–20]

Lord Krishna said:
O Arjuna, hear how practicing yoga with your mind absorbed in Me, taking complete sanctuary in Me, you will be able to know Me completely, without doubt. [1]

Now I shall fully explain to you intellectual and experiential knowledge; upon knowing this, nothing further in the world remains to be known. [2]

Among thousands of humans, hardly one strives for Self-Realization. Of those who do endeavor, scarcely one has realized this Soul-Enlightenment. From these, barely any know Me in truth. [3]

Earth, water, fire, air, ether, mind, intellect, egotism; these are the 8-fold divisions of my nature (prakrti). [4]

Know this O mighty-armed, prakrti (nature) is inferior to my higher prakrti—eternal consciousness—by which this creation is supported. [5]

Know that all beings are generated from these two energies. I am the origin, sustainer, and dissolution of creation. [6]

O Arjuna, there is nothing superior to me; everything that exists is attached to Me like pearls on a thread. [7]

O Arjuna, I am the essential sweet taste in water, the radiance in the Sun and Moon. I am Aum in all the Vedas, the subconscious sound in ether (akasha) and ability in humans. [8]

I am the original fragrance in the earth, the heat in fire, and the vitality in all beings; I am also penance in those performing austerities. [9]

O Arjuna, know Me as the eternal seed of all beings. I am the spiritual intellect of the wise and the prowess of the powerful. [10]

O Arjuna, I am the strength of the strong, without desire or passion, and the energy of procreation that is not contrary to righteousness. [11]

Know that all conditions of nature, goodness (sattwa), passion (rajas), and ignorance (tamas) are created by Me alone; but I am not with them, they are within Me. [12]

The 3 gunas completely delude this universe. This world does not know Me, who is beyond the gunas, eternal. [13]

This divine illusion (maya) of Mine, created by the gunas, is difficult to transcend. Only those who take refuge in Me cross over the maya. [14]

Miscreants, foolish, lowest of humans, their discrimination hoodwinked by maya, following demonic tendencies, do not surrender to Me. [15]

O Arjuna, four kinds of virtuous people offer devotional service to Me; the distressed, the seeker of knowledge, the seeker of material prosperity, and the wise. [16]

Among them, the wise who are always in devotional service to Me, are superior. For I am supremely dear to them and they are dear to Me. [17]

All these people are noble, but I look upon the wise as my very Self. Intent on Self-Realization only, they become one with Me. [18]

After innumerable births, the wise person, seeing all pervaded by Me, realizes Me. Such a great-Soul is very rare. [19]

Those whose minds are distorted by material desires surrender to demigods (devas), following rituals and rites according to their own nature. [20]

Krishna then says something else very interesting: Whatever form a person chooses to worship Me, I make their faith unwavering.

This has many ramifications. Those who worship gods go to the gods. Those who worship God go to God. It might also be interpreted that whatever form of God you worship, God will come to you in that form. [Verse 21–23]

Whatever demigod (deva) a devotee faithfully desires, I make his faith unwavering. [21]

Endowed with that faith, they worship the demigod (devas) and obtain their desires. But it is Me who sanctions the gifts. [22]

For these people of small understanding, the rewards of their desires is temporary. Worshippers of the demigods (devas) obtain the demigods. But my devotees come to Me. [23]

When a person is born, the three *gunas* create, maintain, and dissolve this relative world that Krishna calls *maya* (illusion), because it is not permanent. It is the *gunas* that cause the mind to become deluded into forgetting the eternal God.

When a person begins to desire something that they already are, pairs of opposites are then born. For example, you see a car and are happy. If you want that car—and cannot get it—you become sad.

If you think that obtaining the car will bring lasting happiness, you then try to obtain the car.

But people of virtuous deeds, who take refuge in God, only aim for freedom from all relative bonds caused by the *gunas*. They strive instead for God-Realization or *Brahman*. When a person realizes that all is One, they can then know anything about the relative creation, because they finally see it as a part of themselves. So if you want anything, you must first know the creator of all things.

For the person who knows God in the physical, spiritual, and sacrificial realms of life, God is steadfast in their heart. They remember and know God even at the time of physical death. They know themselves (the Soul) to be eternal. So for them, there is no death; they become imperishable. [Verse 24–30]

These spiritually ignorant people consider me as unmanifest coming into existence. They are unable to understand My imperishable, exalted state. [24]

I am not manifest to all, being veiled by maya. The deluded in this world can not comprehend Me, the unborn and imperishable. [25]

O Arjuna, I know the past, present, and future of all beings, but no one knows Me. [26]

O Arjuna, conqueror of foes, all beings are born in delusion of duality caused by desire and hatred. [27]

But those people performing virtuous acts, whose sins have been completely eradicated, free from delusion of duality, steadfastly engage in devotional service to Me. [28]

Those who strive for liberation from old age and death take refuge in Me; such a person learns about the eternal Soul, the individual Soul, and the entire realm of action and reaction (karma). [29]

Those who realize Me in the physical realm, the divine realm, and as the sacrificial realm, their minds are absorbed in Me, and know Me even at the time of death. [30]

Summary

* God is the creator of the relative world (through the function of the three *gunas*). And God as Soul is in all things. So it is advised for a person to see beyond the impermanence of all things under the influence of the *gunas* to directly experience God.

Exercises

1. How would you best describe your life?;
   a) distressed
   b) seeking knowledge
   c) seeking materialism
   d) serving/worshiping spirit/God
   Are you happy with your life focus or would you like to change the focus?

2. Reflect on any times in the past that you had a strong desire for something or someone and you could not get what you wanted. How did you feel? Did you become impatient, angry, depressed, worried? Did those reactions cause a stressful time in your life? Can you see how by not 'demanding' an outcome, feeling more at one with yourself can prevent extremely stressful situations from arising?

Lord Krishna playing his flute

Chapter 8
How to Attain Salvation

Arjuna asks Krishna to explain in detail some of the concepts Krishna has been speaking about in the past chapters:

What is *Brahman*?

What is *adhyatma*?

What is *karma*?

What is *adhibuta*?

What is *adhidaiva*?

How is God known at the time of death by the wise with steadfast faith on God?

Krishna explains:

1. *Brahman* is the eternal, unbounded, imperishable Supreme—the goal of life—the state of realizing that everything is the same Eternal Soul (God).

   1.2. *Adhyatma* is the embodied soul or the physical manifestation of the Supreme *Brahman*.

   2.3. *Karma* is the process of creation in action.

   3.4. *Adhibuta* is the perishable physical existence.

   4.5. *Adhidaiva* is the Supreme Self or Universal Spirit.

   5.6. Krishna is the *Adhiyajna* (deity of the sacrifice) in the human body.

Those who, at the time of death, remember God, directly merge with God the Eternal. They skip heaven, which is a temporary existence. From heaven, one must again return to earth to continue to achieve Self-Realization. Moreover, the person's last thought just before dying will be attained, because it is the focus of their desire. It has been said that the last wish a person has before dying, will be obtained in their next birth. If a person's last thought is, 'I love that deer,' they will return in their next life as a deer. If their last thought is, 'I wish I was a famous actor,' they will become a famous actor in their next life. This is the theory behind reincarnation and desire.

So powerful is the last thought, that Krishna admonishes all to develop steadfast faith on God so that one's last thought is God.

Now some may say, 'life isn't so bad, I don't mind returning'; however, this is usually said during a positive time and not during some intense suffering. Moreover, as one becomes more infirm in later life—suffering from health and financial issues, loneliness, or fear of dying—they are likely to see the issue differently. A person who is unable to feel the suffering of humanity may say that they do not see any problems with life. But the compassionate will find it hard to always feel truly happy as long as there are cries for help somewhere on the earth.

Still, this admonition does not mean that living life for God and focusing on God makes this appear to be a cold and dismal place; quite the opposite. One can indeed enjoy life in moderation and see God's hand in all things. It is only when enjoyment becomes so great that a person forgets the author of the creation and the giver of the joy. It is this what Krishna warns about.

So Krishna repeats, from various angles, the same message. Those who meditate on God, who see God as beyond the smallest, beyond the darkness, with unflinching mind and possessed of devotion, fixing the *prana* (life-breath) between the brows through *yogic* practice, will attain the Supreme Divine Being.

In layman's terms, Krishna is saying that any doubt, fear, anxiety, anger or other unwarranted emotion is an impurity, an aberration of a peaceful mind at one with God. Some may use the term 'evil' to describe any thought or feeling other than a godly one, because it causes upset in mind and body in the form of stress and disease. This microscopic insight into human nature reveals the need to be ever vigilant, ever self analytical, to ever refine the mind and heart toward a purer and more peaceful state of being. The implications of this idea are astounding. Imagine that every time you want to blame another person for something, instead you look inside to see if you have removed all impurities or faults. An applicable expression is that *'People who live in glass houses should not throw stones'* or *'every time you point a finger in blame, three fingers point back at you.'*

If everything in creation is a part of the eternal Self, then any imperfection or fault that is seen exists in the person who sees the fault in another. The only way to purify or rectify that fault is to look within and purify oneself. [Verse 1–11]

Arjuna said:
O Krishna, what is Brahman (cosmic Soul)? What is individual Soul? What is karma (action/reaction)? What is the physical realm, and what is the divine realm? [1]

O Krishna, who is the Lord of sacrifice within the body? How does it dwell there and how can this be known at the time of death by the self-controlled? [2]

Lord Krishna said:
The supreme, imperishable reality is Brahman. Its embodied nature is the self (adhyatman). Action that causes the development of material bodies is called karma (fruitive actions). [3]

O Arjuna, the perishable world is called the physical realm (adhibhuta), the eternal unmanifest is the underlying foundation of all the demigods (adhidaivata), and in the body, I am the Lord of all sacrifices (Adhiyajna). [4]

The person who remembers Me at the time of their death, rises and becomes one with Me. There is no doubt about this. [5]

O Arjuna, the last thing a person thinks about in their final moment, they become [in their next life], due to their absorption in that thought. [6]

Therefore, think of Me constantly and fight, offering your mind and intellect to Me, and definitely you shall attain Me without doubt. [7]

O Arjuna, by continually remembering the resplendent Supreme Being, with individual and universal Soul united, a person realizes (God). [8]

The person who thinks upon the omniscient, ancient ruler, smaller than an atom yet sustainer of all; of unimaginable form, radiant like the Sun, and beyond ignorance. [9]

> *At the time of death, one who meditates on Him with concentrated mind, full devotion, and fixes their life breath (prana) between the eyebrows, will realize that eternal God. [10]*
>
> *That path which the realizers of Veda speak of as imperishable, that which the great renunciants (sanyasins) merge by practicing Brahmacharya, I shall summarize for you. [11]*

Krishna then shares the secret of how to become awake to one's Soul. He says a person can develop *yogic* concentration by:

- Closing all the gates to their senses

- Confining the mind in the heart

- Fixing *prana* at *ajna chakra* (ie, focusing the eyes upward between the brows)

- Uttering the sound *Aum* (the first word of the universe) and meditating on God. (This can also be interpreted as saying any name of God.)

Krishna says that those who remember God daily, constantly at each and every moment of life will easily attain God as their supreme goal. And having attained God and realizing the eternal kingdom, there is no rebirth, because there is no desire to experience anything worldly.

Krishna next gives some perspective on creation and time. A day for Brahma, the creator of the universe, lasts for 1,000 *yugas* (cycles or ages); his night lasts for another 1,000 *yugas*. Those who have experienced this knowledge are the true knowers of day and night. (1,000 *yugas* is called a *kalpa*, and lasts for 4,320,000,000 earthly years)

There are a few points of discussion regarding these statements by Krishna. First, human life is but a drop in the ocean of time. Our life on earth is infinitesimal; let us spend it wisely. Second, just as a day of Brahma is so vast by our standards of time and our lifetime passes in a wink of an eye, through steadfast devotion, we can still come to know God during that short time. From this viewpoint, life becomes more precious.

When Brahma's night begins, he goes to sleep and the creation ends for another *kalpa*. It is withdrawn back into Brahma. When it is Brahma's day, he awakes again to create creation.

According to Vedic texts, when God wanted to create the universe, He created Brahma and instructed him to do the job for Him. Brahma felt the need to go into deep meditation to understand his source (God) and his mission (to create the universe). When Brahma achieved realization, seeing that everything comes from God, he was then able to create the universe. He created it from his thoughts. [Verse 12–19]

Withdrawing the senses from sense objects and steadying the mind within the heart, fixed in Self-Realization with the life breath (prana) in the head, engaged in the practice of union of individual and universal Soul (yoga). [12]

Uttering the eternal monosyllable, Aum, and continuously remembering Me, thus they relinquish their body and achieve the supreme goal. [13]

O Arjuna, whosoever remembers Me constantly without interruption, I am easy to attain because of their constant devotion. [14]

The great souls who have reached Me do not undergo transitory rebirth of misery. [15]

O Arjuna, the inhabitants of the world, from the most evolved, Brahma's sphere downwards, are subject to the cycle of birth and death. By taking refuge in Me, O Arjuna, there is no rebirth. [16]

Those who know that a day for Brahma consists of 4,320,000,000 years, as does the duration of one of his nights, are knowers of day and night. [17]

At the onset of Brahma's day, all creatures are created from the unmanifest, and at the arrival of night, they merge into that which is called unmanifest. [18]

O Arjuna, these innumerable beings continually take birth at the beginning of his day, and disappear at the advent of his night, and again manifesting automatically upon the start of the next day. [19]

Now, yet another fascinating point is made. When creation is destroyed during Brahma's sleep, there is a form of creation that is unmanifest: every creature and *deva* are manifest anew, again and again, in each creation.

But higher than this is the ultimate unmanifest—that which has no form and is unbounded. This is what has been described earlier as the Supreme Imperishable. Attaining this state, there is no rebirth even when the next new creation is begun. Thus, we are given an awe-inspiring view of the Vedic notion of time, creation, birth, death, and reincarnation, of the temporal nature of heaven, and what eternal salvation truly means.

Seeing our place in such a vast and incomprehensible play and among a cast of great characters can help us feel humble. We can see how little understanding and power we have over things in life beyond doing our best to use our God-given gifts to help others. This view also offers solace and inspiration rather than despair, because we know that if we follow the secret teachings of Krishna, we will improve our lives. We can develop a life of devotion to God and help God's children and the earth to the best of our ability.

Finally, Krishna shares the secrets about when we will depart from the earth (leave our bodies) for God, and when we return again for rebirth. We learn that Eternal Salvation is attained when leaving the body, through fire, light, and in the daytime during the waxing moon cycle (bright fortnight or *shukla*) in the six months of the sun's northern course. Rebirth occurs upon leaving the body during smoke and at night during the waning moon cycle (dark fortnight or *Krishna* [meaning dark in this context]) in the six months of the sun's southern course.

With all these secrets about how to attain unshakable devoted faith in God, Krishna admonishes Arjuna to aim for this highest goal of life—*Brahman* or Self-Realization so that he can live in that imperishable state. [Verse 20–28]

But there is another unmanifest that is eternal and superior to this relative unmanifest (of Brahma), that is never destroyed even when all beings perish. [20]

That unmanifest that is described as imperishable is called the supreme goal; having realized, one never is reborn. That is my supreme abode. [21]

O Arjuna, that supreme Self, in whom all beings live and by whom all things are pervaded, can be achieved only by whole-hearted devotion. [22]

O Arjuna, now I'll explain about the time for passing from this world [i.e. death of the body] when the yogis realize liberation and the time of death when they will have rebirth. [23]

Yogis attain liberation when they leave through Fire (agni), light (Jyoti), daytime (Aha), during the waxing Moon (Shukla), the 6-month northern course of the sun (between winter and summer solstices) (Uttataryanam) [24]

When Yogis pass from this world through smoke (Dhuma), night (Ratri), during the waning Moon (Krsna), the 6-month course of the Sun (between summer and winter solstice), after remaining in heaven for some time, undergo rebirth. [25]

These are eternal light and dark paths of the universe. Through one a yogi realizes liberation, and through the other they repeatedly return. [26]

O Arjuna, by knowing these paths, yogis are never deluded. Therefore, O Arjuna, always be engaged in Self-Realization. [27]

Whatever meritorious rewards are promised in the Vedas, in ritual sacrifices, in practicing austerities, or in charitable giving, the yogi, transcends them all to realize the supreme primeval abode. [28]

Exercises

1. Krishna said doubt, fear, anxiety, anger, or other unwarranted emotions prevent a mind in peace, at one with God. For the next few days, scan your brain whenever you remember to see what you are thinking about. While getting ready for school or work, in the shower, brushing your teeth, preparing or eating a meal, walking or driving, waiting for someone; browse your thoughts like channel surfing—what thoughts do you see? What conversations are being presented—angry, worried, joyful, sacred? The thought stories are like air—negative thoughts pollute your awareness and harmonious thoughts create fresh air. If you are seeing negative thoughts, try instantly changing to something

harmonious; a happy or spiritual song, a mantra or prayer, a pleasant event, a loving person, think of your life purpose, or how you can best help others. By continually scanning your thoughts in daily life and consciously switching to harmonious thoughts, you will gradually exercise your mind to think more constructive thoughts and thereby feel more peace in life.

2. Review your emotions; is there anyone you blame for something that happened to you? Do you label that person phony, uncaring, egotistic; maybe something they did or did not do or say prevented you from experiencing an outcome you wished for? Now look within to see where you might be blocking others or yourself with your thoughts and actions—but do not judge yourself. It is not an easy exercise to see and admit one's own short comings. If you can admit it, it makes you humble; try to forgive yourself and the other person too. Instead of dwelling on the issue, switch your focus to your God-gifts and how you can better share your gifts with others. Do you feel lighter, more harmonious from the shift to positive emotions and action?

3. This is the second chapter that discusses reincarnation. For those new to the idea, it is a good time to review your initial thoughts and journaling to see if you have gained any new insights.

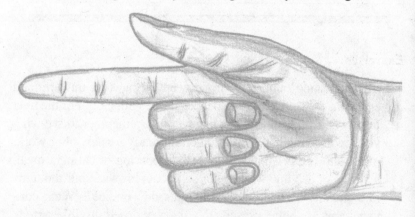

When you point a finger in blame, you have three fingers pointing back at you. This is a modern expression that relates to this ancient spiritual principle; what you see in others is merely a reflection of what is in your own self.

Chapter 9
Secrets to Attaining Self-Realization

In this chapter Lord Krishna shares the secret of how wisdom and realization together can help a person be freed from illness (bondage, evil, or all impurities). He says this *yoga* is the king of sciences, king of secrets, and the supreme purifier.

The way to know this is by directly experiencing a life of righteousness or *dharma*. It is easily performed, and it is timeless and changeless.

People who have no faith in this *dharma* or science of Self-Realization go through continual rebirth without ever knowing God. But those who know God, know that God is unmanifest—pervading all things. So all people reside in the all-pervading God, but God does not reside in them in the sense that God is beyond anything manifest. Just as all people reside in the mist of a foggy day, all people reside within unmanifest God. Just as the air and ether are everywhere, so is God all pervading. Yet God is also beyond air and ether.

At the end of creation, all beings return to God's nature (*prakrti)*, and at the beginning of a new cycle, God creates them again. God is unattached to the actions of starting and dissolving creations, since God is beyond all manifestation. To the degree that people desire intellectual knowledge, power, beauty, wealth—all things of the small, temporal creation, instead of desiring to become more intimate with God, is the same degree that they are deluded about God's eternal, Divine nature. So it is said they behave like monsters and demons. However those who know God as the imperishable source of all creation, ever lovingly worship God and ever sing His glories.

Lord Krishna cites various forms in which God is worshipped—through religious rituals, in fire sacrifices, by honoring departed ancestors, with medicinal herbs, and through the recitation of *mantras*. God is the ritual, God is the act of offering the ritual, and God is that which is offered in the ritual. In short, everything is God when anything is offered in God's name.

Krishna says that God is the parent, grandparent, child, sustainer, the One, the *Aum*, the *Vedas*. God is everything in existence. God is the way, the friend, the supporter, the witness, the home, the refuge, the source, the lover, the enemy—because even in hatred—a person, who always thinks of God and always pictures God in their mind, attains God.

God is the giver of heat and cold, rain and drought, death and immortality, manifest and unmanifest. Those who make an offering to God, and partake in the remnant of the offering (*prashad* or *soma*) become purified. They see more of the real nature of God than do others.

Those who pray for heaven attain this state for a while. Returning to earth after their merits have expired, they continue to be ruled by the cycle of birth and death. For those who worship God and meditate on God without any desire for anything, continually loving God as its own reward and devoting acts to help God's children as its own reward, God provides all their basic necessities in life and carries their burdens.

Whatever or whomever a person worships; they go to that realm upon death. Those who worship the lesser gods, go to their realm. But only those who worship the one God will go to God's realm upon death.

Regardless what a person devotedly offers to God in worship, be it a flower, fruit, or water, if it is offered with a pure heart, God accepts. Whatever we do, eat, speak, or think, should be offered with a pure heart to God. [Verse 1–28]

Lord Krishna said:
Now I am explaining to you who are without envy, this most secret wisdom, the knowledge of realization, which after knowing, you will be liberated from the miseries of material life. [1]

This is the king of all wisdom, the king of all secrets, the supreme purifying righteousness, able to be perceived through experiential realization, most joyous to perform, and eternal. [2]

O Arjuna, those with no faith on this path of devotional service cannot attain me. They return to the birth and death cycle in this material world. [3]

By My unmanifest form, the entire world is pervaded by me. All living beings dwell in Me, but I do not dwell in them. [4]

While I create and protect all beings, they do not dwell in Me, nor do I dwell in them. [5]

Just as the wind blows everywhere, it always remains within space; in the same way, all living beings always exist within Me. [6]

O Arjuna, all beings enter into My nature at the end of a 4,320,000,000 cycle (kalpa), and after another cycle (of equal length), I create them again. [7]

Ruling over my nature (prakriti), I create all innumerable living beings again and again, according to their nature. [8]

O Arjuna, these actions do not bind me; I am neutral and unattached to all these actions. [9]

O Arjuna, with Me presiding over all nature, manifesting all moving and non-moving entities, the cosmic creation is repeated continually. [10]

Unaware of My spiritual nature, foolish people disregard Me dwelling in human form. [11]

These bewildered people of vain desires, vain actions, vain knowledge, and vain understanding; they assume an atheistic and demonic nature. [12]

However, O Arjuna, those great souls who have taken refuge in My Divine nature, perform devotional service to Me with focused mind, and knowing Me as the eternal cause of all creation. [13]

Ever singing My glory, always striving with great determination, bowing down before Me, these great souls are ever worshiping Me with loving devotion. [14]

Others perform the sacrifice of cultivating spiritual wisdom by worshiping God as the one without a second, as duality, and as manifold forms. [15]

I am Kratu (the 7 fire rituals), I am Yajna (the 5 daily sacrifices), I am Svadha (the oblations offered to departed ancestors), I am Aushadham (the healing herb), I am mantra, I am ghee, I am the fire, and I am the act of offering. [16]

I am the father of the universe, the mother, the grandfather, the progenitor, the essence to be known, the purifier, and the symbol Aum, the Rig, Sama, and Yajur Vedas. [17]

I am the path, the supporter, the lord, the witness, the refuge, the guardian, the well-wisher, the creation, the maintaining, the dissolution, the reservoir, and the eternal cause. [18]

O Arjuna, I give heat, send forth and withhold rain, I alone am immorality and death. I am all that is unmanifest and manifest. [19]

The knowers of the 3 Vedas who, purified from worshipping me and drinking soma, pray for heavenly goals, worship me indirectly. They attain the celestial region of Indra's planet where they enjoy celestial delights. [20]

Having enjoyed the vast heavenly spheres, exhausting their earned spiritual merit, return to the mortal world; thus following the doctrine of righteousness in the 3 Vedas, craving for worldly pleasures, they continue in the cycle of birth and death. [21]

Those who desire My eternal association and nothing else, meditating on Me with exclusive devotion; to these devotees, I carry their burdens and provide all their basic necessities. [22]

O Arjuna, those who devotedly worship different demigods with faith, they also worship me, but in an unauthorized manner. [23]

I am alone the enjoyer and lord of all sacrifice; but they do not know Me in reality, thus they revolve in the cycle of rebirth. [24]

The worshippers of the demigods go to the gods; worshippers of the ancestors go to the ancestors, spirit worshippers go to the spirits, but My worshippers come to Me. [25]

Whoever with loving devotion, offers Me a leaf, flower, fruit, or water, I affectionately accept that love-offering from that pure-hearted person. [26]

O Arjuna, whatever you do, whatever you eat, whatever you offer in sacrifice, whatever you give in charity, whatever austerities you do, all that you do; make them an offering to Me. [27]

In this way you will become free from auspicious and inauspicious results from the binding of actions; with your Soul devotedly in renunciation through yoga, liberated, you will come to Me. [28]

This type of offering frees a person from the bonds of actions that yield the fruits of 'good' and 'bad' and liberate the person to be one with God.

Krishna says,
I have no favorites among people; no hated or beloved by Me. But those who worship Me with devotion, they are in Me and I am in them. [Verse 29]

> *I am the same to all beings; neither friend nor foe to Me; but those who devotedly worship Me, they are in Me and I am in them. [29]*

Even if the most wicked of people worship God in this way, they would be regarded as a 'good' person for their resolute mind. That person quickly becomes a righteous Soul and attains eternal peace.

Anyone, man or woman, rich or poor, even the outcast, or those thought to be inferior to other humans, can realize Brahman (God is One). No one is barred from Self-Realization.

So Krishna ends the chapter reminding us of the method how to attain Self-Realization:

Fill your mind with God in devoted worship.

Steadfastly unite your heart with God alone Who is the Supreme Goal, and you shall realize God.

This is the secret science of mysticism as taught to humans by Lord Krishna. [Verse 30 – 34]

> *Even if a wicked person worships Me with undivided devotion, they are to be considered saintly, because they are properly resolved. [30]*
>
> *Quickly they become righteous and attain eternal peace. O Arjuna, know that My devotees never perish. [31]*
>
> *O Arjuna, even those born of lower classes, by taking refuge in Me, attain to the supreme goal. [32]*
>
> *So what need is there to speak about the devotees, the pious and royal sages. Having reached this transitory world of misery, engage in devotional worship to Me. [33]*

> *Keep Me ever in your mind, be My devotee, worship Me, bow to Me. Through uniting your heart with Me and having Me as the Supreme Goal, you will realize Me. [34]*

Exercise

This chapter focuses on attaining Self-Realization, but many people wonder what this term really means. They ask for a description of the 'experience'. However, since experiencing Self-Realization or Soul is beyond all worldly boundaries, the short answer is that it cannot be described using words; it can only be experienced. But how can you experience what is beyond experience? It is said that your *Soul awareness experiences itself*; it awakens to itself.

Has it ever dawned on you the sun was out, your throat was no longer sore, or that the lawn mower shut off some time ago and you are just now aware of the silence or chirping of the birds; or you listen to your conscience and your mind becomes settled? When the friction (physical or mental) disappears and inner awareness real- izes the restored peace and harmony, these are metaphors for eternal awareness awakening to itself.

The experience of Self-Realization is said to be 'blissful', but it is a bliss not caused by anything external, including the mind, feelings, or senses. This is why it cannot be grasped intellectually. However, when one is living in balance/harmony with nature, serving others and the earth, meditating or praying, trying to love and not harm anyone or anything in thought, word, or action, they feel a sense of inner purpose and content- ment. This is what it means to fill your mind with God. This is the growth of Soul aware- ness. Reflect on times you have experienced this and consider what you can do to further cultivate it in your life now.

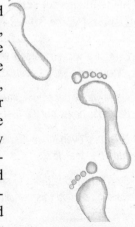

God's footprints, when carrying the weary

Chapter 10
How to Find God in Daily Life

Krishna reviews God's position as permeating everything, yet being beyond all creation including the gods; eternal and unmanifest. Those who know this are not deluded in life.

All attributes come from God, including intelligence, wisdom, forgiveness, truthfulness, serenity, equanimity, contentment, austerity, and benevolence. All experiences come from God, including pleasure and pain, birth and death, fame and infamy, fear and fearlessness. All gods, people, animals, nature, spirits, and demons arise from God. In short, everything in the entire creation comes from God and from nowhere else. Nothing is beyond God.

Arjuna now asks Krishna to relate all the forms of manifestation and attributes that God has created of Himself. Then he asks Krishna to tell him what form of God he should meditate on.

Krishna says that, above all things, God is the eternal Self that resides in the heart of all beings. He is Vishnu, the radiant sun; Marichi, the chief of the winds; the moon; Sama Veda; Indra's mind; the consciousness in all living things. He is Shankara; the lord of wealth; the fire god; Meru, the king of the mountains. God is Brihaspati, the high priest; Skanda, the head of the generals; the ocean and chief of all waters. He is Brigu, the greatest seer; Aum, the first word; japa, silent repetition of sacred texts; chief of sacrifices, Himalaya, head of immovable objects. God is Ashwattha, chief of the trees; Gandharvas, chief of the celestial musicians; and Kapila, the sage and head of all perfected beings.

He is the head of horses, born of nectar, lord of the elephants, and monarch among humans. God is the thunderbolt among weapons, head of the cows. The source of all offspring, and the chief snake, Vasuki. Krishna goes on listing examples of God's Divine manifestations. He is time, the cause of all action and fruits thereof, death, fame, prosperity, speech, memory, intelligence, forgiveness, the seasons and so on. In short, God is the essence and chief of all worldly things. There is no end to God's manifestations since God is always creating new forms. [Verse 1–42]

Lord Krishna said:
O mighty armed, listen again to My supreme teachings, which I will speak for your welfare, as you delight in them. [1]

Neither the demigods (devas) or the great seers (rishis) know My eternal origin because I am the source of these celestials and great sages. [2]

One who knows Me as birthless, without beginning, and the Supreme Lord of the universe, they alone are not misguided among humans, and are freed from all sins. [3]

Spiritual intelligence, wisdom, non-delusion, forgiveness, truth, sense control, control of the mind, happiness and sadness, birth and death, fear and fearlessness. [4]

Non-violence, equanimity, contentment, penance, charity, fame and infamy; these are the different states of beings that arise from Me only. [5]

The seven great seers (rishis) [Marici, Atri, Angiras, Pulastya, Pulaha, Kratu, Vasishtha], and before them, the four other great sages, and the Manus, all were born of My mind, and all beings descend from them. [6]

One who knows this reality, My various manifestations and My yoga power, realizes permanent union of individual and eternal Soul. There is no doubt in this regard. [7]

I am the original cause of all; everything emanates from Me. Knowing this, the wise worship Me with devotional ecstasy. [8]

With their minds fully focused on Me, their life absorbed in Me, perpetually enlightening one another and continuing to sing My glories, they rejoice and are contented. [9]

To those devoted and dedicated to Me, I give that yoga of wisdom by which they come to Me. [10]

Out of compassion for them, I, dwelling in their heart, destroy the darkness born of ignorance, with the radiant light of wisdom. [11]

Arjuna said:
You are the Supreme Brahman, the Supreme Truth and most sacred; all the exalted sages, Narada, Asita, Devala, and Vyasa, have declared You as the Eternal,

Self-Effulgent being—the original Lord of all gods, omnipresent. Now You personally are declaring this to me. [12-13]

O Krishna, all You have told me I accept as fact. O God, neither the demigods nor demons understand your divine manifestations. [14]

O Supreme one, O Origin of all origins, O Lord of all beings, O God of gods, O Lord of the universe, You alone know Yourself by Yourself. [15]

Please tell me in detail of Your divine powers by which You pervade all the worlds. [16]

O Krishna, how can I come to know you through constant meditation? In what forms are You to be meditated? [17]

O Krishna, please tell me again the details of Your mighty abilities and glories. I am never satiated from hearing these words of nectar. [18]

Lord Krishna said:
O Arjuna, I shall tell you My divine manifestations, but only those that are prominent, for My opulence is unlimited. [19]

O Arjuna, I reside in the heart of all creatures, and I am the beginning, middle and end of all creatures. [20]

I am Vishnu of the 12 Adityas, I am the Sun of the luminaries, among the winds, I am Marichi, and among constellations I am the Moon. [21]

Of the Vedas I am Sama Veda, of the demigods (devas) I am Indra. Of the senses I am the mind, and of all living creatures I am consciousness. [22]

Of the Rudras I am Shiva, of the Yakshas and Rakshasas I am Kuvera, the lord of wealth; of the Vasus I am Agni-fire and of mountains I am Meru. [23]

O Arjuna, know me to be Brihaspati, the chief priest, of generals I am Skanda, of waters I am the ocean. [24]

Among the great sages (rishis) I am Brighu, of words I am the monosyllable Aum, of sacrifices I am the silent repetition of mantras (japa), of immoveable things I am the Himalaya mountains. [25]

Of trees I am the sacred Peepal (Ashwatta), of divine seers (rishis) I am Narada, of the celestial musicians (Gandharvas) I am Chitraratha, of the perfected ones I am sage Kapila. [26]

Among horses I am Uchchaisrava, born of nectar (amrit); of lordly elephants I am Airavata; and among humans I am the king. [27]

I am the thunderbolt among weapons, of cows I am the wish-fulfilling Kamadhuk, I am Cupid (Candarpa) cause of offspring, and among serpents I am Vasuki. [28]

I am Ananta among snakes, I am Varuna among aquatic creatures, I am Aryama (minister of justice) among ancestors, I am Yama (lord of death) among rulers [29]

Of the Daityas I am Prahlada, of measurements I am time, of all the animals, I am the lion, of birds I am Garuda. [30]

Of the purifiers I am wind, of warriors I am Rama, of fish I am Makara (shark), and of rivers I am Ganga. [31]

O Arjuna, I alone am the creator, sustainer, and dissolver of all creation. Of knowledge I am Self-knowledge, and of arguments I am truth-seeking (Vada). [32]

Among letters I am the first letter A, among compound words Dvandva (the dual word), I am eternal time and the four-faced Brahma. [33]

I am all-devouring death, I am the first birth of the six manifestations of all creatures; of females I am fame, prosperity, speech, memory, intelligence, patience, and forgiveness. [34]

Of the Sama Veda I am the Brihat-sama, of mantras I am Gayatri, of the months I am the fall harvest, and among seasons I am spring. [35]

Among deceivers I am gambling, I am the glory of the glorious, I am victory, perseverance, I am the nobility of the noble. [36]

I am Vasudeva among the Vrishnis, I am Arjuna among the Pandavas, I am Vyasadeva among the saints, I am Usana among the great scholars. [37]

Of disciplinarians I am the rod, of those seeking success I am strategy, I am silence among secrets, and I am wisdom of the wise. [38]

O Arjuna, whatever is the essence of beings that I also am. Nothing exists that is moving or stationary without Me. [39]

O Arjuna, there is no end of My divine manifestations. But I have only summarized the vastness of my divine forms. [40]

Whatever is glorious, beautiful, or powerful, know that all these manifestations arise from Me, but are an iota of My splendor. [41]

O Arjuna, what need is there for you to know more details? Alone, I exist supporting this entire universe situated in a portion of my Self. [42]

Exercise

This chapter spotlights God existing in all things in material creation. Because this conversation originally took place in India thousands of years ago, the terminology is geared to Arjuna, his religion and culture. But we can easily transpose more universal terms for these aspects of nature. Rather than get caught in the semantics of calling fire the god Agni, we can practice seeing God in fire, or at least being grateful for God creating fire.

- As you move through your day, notice the things you are grateful for (friendly co-workers, delicious lunch, challenging opportunities). Try to appreciate beauty and grace in all people, buildings, nature, etc.

- Create a gratitude journal. Each night before going to bed, review your day and write down the things you were grateful for during that day (eg, sunshine, home-cooked dinner, your health, your family, your baby daughter learning a new word).

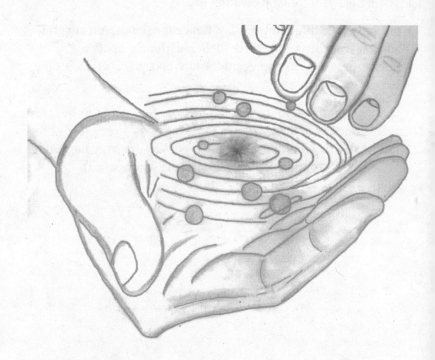

God permeates everything, yet is beyond all creation

Chapter 11
Seeing God's Universal Form

Arjuna becomes bolder now, inspired by hearing all the forms of God, he now asks if it is possible if he can 'see' the universal form of God that shows His infinite manifestations. Krishna agrees and reveals His universal form to Arjuna, but Krishna says that humans cannot normally have such a vision. Thus, Arjuna is temporarily given Divine sight. It is a beautiful description to read of the countless faces, beautiful garlands, and fragrances, radiant like a thousand suns, seeing the entire universe resting in the God's body. Within Krishna's body are all gods and seers (*rishis*), sages, and Divine beings. Arjuna also sees all the demons being sucked into the mouths of God [see illustration on page 124].

Krishna then explains the purpose for His manifestation on earth at this time. God is here to remove the unrighteousness that has begun to gain the upper hand in the world. The armies that Arjuna is fighting will die at the will of God—even if Arjuna does not choose to fight—because they are the cause of *adharma* (unrighteousness).

So Krishna tells Arjuna that it is better that he fights, knowing as he does that Arjuna's side will win and that the others will be killed. He tells him to cast off his sadness and delusions about killing those who cannot be killed (souls do not die).

Arjuna is now quite emotional, seeing such a Divine sight and hearing about the future that God holds for his enemy. He praises Krishna even while shaking in awe over all the events he is experiencing. Arjuna then cites a beautiful prayer:

In whatever manner I may have been disrespectful to Thee,
While joking, walking, sleeping, sitting, eating, alone or with others,
I beg you please forgive any transgression I may have made.
I see that you are the cause of creation and beyond it,
The only one worthy to worship.

Now, please, I cannot bear the weight of this Divine vision.
Please return to your human form of Krishna again. Take pity on me.

Krishna says that no study of the *Vedas*, sacrifice, charity, ritual, or austerity, can give a person such a vision as this. Not even the gods can see this form of Me. Only through single-hearted devotion can one see this universal form of Mine. Do not be frightened, I shall return to my Krishna form.

The person who devotes their works for God and makes God their highest goal is free from attachment to material things and bears no enmity toward any creature. That person alone becomes one with Me. [Verse 1–55]

Arjuna said:
By You mercifully sharing these supremely mystical teachings regarding Self-knowledge with me, You have dispelled my illusions. [1]

O Krishna, I have heard the details of creation and dissolution of all creatures, as well as of Your eternal glories. [2]

O Krishna, as You have described your ultimate Self, this is so. O Supreme One, I wish to see Your divine form. [3]

O Lord, if you feel I am worthy to see that form, then please show me your ultimate Self, O Krishna. [4]

Lord Krishna said:
O Arjuna, behold My various celestial forms with hundreds and thousands of varied colors and shapes. [5]

O Arjuna, see the 12 Adityas, the 8 Vasus, the 11 Shivas, the Ashwini twins, the 49 Maruts, behold many wonders that were never seen before. [6]

O Arjuna, see in My body the entire universe and all that is moving and unmoving, and whatever else you desire to see. [7]

But with your eyes you cannot see Me. So I grant you divine sight. Behold My omnipotent, unified power. [8]

Sanjaya said:
O King, having spoken thus, Lord Krishna, the supreme God of Self-Realization, showed his transcendental, omnipotent universal form to Arjuna. [9]

Revealing His innumerable wondrous sights, innumerable mouths and eyes, decorated with many celestial ornaments, and armed with many celestial weapons. [10]

Gloriously attired and garlanded, anointed with divine fragrant perfumes, this was an amazing and radiant form of God, infinite and everywhere. [11]

If the effulgence of a thousand suns were to shine simultaneously in the sky, that may resemble the effulgence of that great form of God. [12]

Then Arjuna saw the entire universe with its many divisions, all situated in this universal form of Lord Krishna, the God of all gods. [13]

Then Arjuna became overwhelmed with awe; his hair stood on end. Bowing to Krishna he folded his hands and spoke to Him. [14]

Arjuna said:
O God, in Your body I see all the demigods and a multitude of manifold beings; Lord Brahma seated on the lotus flower; Lord Shiva and many sages and divine serpents. [15]

O Lord of the universe, O Universal Form, I see Your unlimited form with innumerable arms, bellies, faces, and eyes; with no beginning, middle, or end. [16]

I see You in all directions, with crowns, maces, and discus (chakras); illuminating resplendently everywhere like a blazing fire and radiant suns; difficult to view and immeasurable. [17]

You are the Supreme Eternal Truth to be realized. You are the Supreme Refuge of the universe; you are Eternal Path of Duty (dharma), You are the Ancient One. I am convinced of all this. [18]

I see You without beginning, middle, or end, with infinite energy, with unlimited arms, with eyes like the Sun and Moon, with blazing fire in Your mouths, warming this universe with Your own glorious resplendence. [19]

The space between heaven, earth, and all the directions are pervaded by You alone. O greatest of all, by seeing this wonderful and terrible form of Yours, the three worlds tremble with fear. [20]

Verily, all the hosts of demigods (devas) are entering into You. Some in fear, some praising you with folded hands. The great sages (Rishis and Siddhas) are worshiping you, singing hymns of Your glory (svasti) from the Vedic scriptures. [21]

The Rudras, Adityas, Vasus, Sadhyas, Vishvas, Ashwins, Maruts, Ushmapas, Gandharvas, Yakshas, Asuras, Siddhas, are all looking at You in wonder. [22]

O Mighty armed, seeing Your immeasurable form, with myriad faces and eyes, many arms, legs, and feet, manifold bellies and many terrifying teeth; all the planets tremble in fear and so do I. [23]

O Krishna, seeing You touching the sky, radiating many colors, with mouths open wide and large blazing eyes; verily I am trembling within myself, unable to maintain my fortitude or equilibrium. [24]

Just by seeing your mouth with terrible teeth, blazing like the fires of universal destruction, I know not the cardinal directions nor do I find any peace. O Krishna, Lord of all gods, O refuge of the universe, have mercy on me. [25]

All the sons of Dhritarashtra, with the multifarious armies of monarchs, Bhishma, Dronacharya, Sutaputra (Karna), as well as our main warriors, are rushing forward into Your mouths, terrible with long teeth and fearful to see. Some are seen with their heads smashed, sticking between the teeth. [26, 27]

Just as many rivers run into the ocean, so these kings are entering into Your fiery mouths from all directions. [28]

As moths rush into a blazing fire and perish, so all these armies are speedily rushing into Your mouths only to perish. [29]

O Krishna, You are swallowing and devouring all these people from all directions in Your fiery mouths, covering the universe with Your immeasurable radiance, and scorching the worlds. [30]

Please tell me who You are in this terrible form. I praise you O Lord, be merciful to me. O Primeval One, I wish to clearly know You because I cannot understand Your purpose. [31]

Lord Krishna said:
I am the terrible Time, destroyer of all creatures in all worlds. Even without you, all these opposing armies will be destroyed. [32]

Therefore, arise for battle O Arjuna. You will gain fame by conquering the enemy and enjoy a flourishing kingdom. All these warriors have already been slain by Me due to previous arrangements. You are only the instrument in this battle. [33]

Drona, Bhishma, Jayadratha, Karna, and other brave warriors are already slain by Me. So kill them without distress. Just fight and you will conquer your enemies in battle. [34]

Sanjaya said:
Hearing Lord Krishna's admonition, Arjuna, wearing a crown, with folded hands, and trembling, offered his respects with a fearful heart. With a faltering voice, he spoke to Krishna again. [35]

Arjuna said:
O Krishna, it is true that the entire universe is exalted by singing your glories. Out of fear, the demons (Rakshasas) flee in all four directions and the perfected beings (Siddhas) offer adoring praise to You. [36]

Why should they not offer their respects to You, O Soul of souls; the creator of Brahma? O Infinite one, O Lord of the gods! O Refuge of the universe and most worshipable, You are imperishable, the manifest and unmanifest, and beyond them. [37]

You are the original Lord, the eternal being. You are the supreme refuge of the universe; the knower and the known; the supreme abode. The universe is permeated by You alone. [38]

You are the wind (Vayu), death (Yama), fire (Agni), water (Varuna), the Moon, Brahma, and Vishnu. I offer You devotional obeisance, thousands and thousands of times. Again, my respectful obeisance to you again and again. [39]

O all my salutations to You; from the front, from the back; I offer obeisance to You from all sides as well. O You of eternal energy and infinite power. You completely permeate the entire creation. Thus you are everything. [40]

In the past I have address You as 'O Krishna', 'O Yadava' 'O my friend', due to delusion or affection, without knowing your glories and universal form. [41]

O infallible one, whatever disrespect may have occurred jokingly while playing, resting, sitting, eating, alone or with others, all these things I pray You please forgive me. [42]

You are the father of the moving and unmoving creation, and its object of worship and spiritual master. You are incomparable; no one is equal to You; how can anyone excel You? [43]

Thus, prostrating my body in devotion, O Krishna I beg Your forgiveness as a father forgives a son, a friend their dear friend, and a beloved one their love. So too O Krishna, forgive me. [44]

O Krishna, while I am enthralled to see Your universal form, my mind is agitated with fear. O God of gods, therefore have mercy on me and show me Your human form again. [45]

O Krishna, I wish to see You as before, with crown, mace, and discus. O thousand armed Universal Form, do assume Your familiar four-armed form. [46]

Lord Krishna said:
O Arjuna, pleased with you I have revealed My universal form by My own power of yoga. This radiant, infinite, primeval has not been seen by anyone but you. [47]

O Arjuna, not by studying Vedas, by sacrifice, charity, rituals, or severe austerities can I be seen in this form in the material world except by you. [48]

Do not be frightened or bewildered by seeing My universal form. Get rid of your fear and with gladdened heart, see My former form again. [49]

Sanjaya said:
Having thus spoken to Arjuna, Lord Krishna showed His four-armed form, then finally His 2-armed form; thus pacifying the frightened Arjuna. [50]

Arjuna said:
O Krishna, seeing Your beautiful two-armed form, my mind is pacified and I have recovered myself. [51]

Lord Krishna said:
This form of mine that you have witnessed is rarely ever seen; even the demigods ever aspire to see this form. [52]

My form cannot be seen from studying Vedas, by austerities, charity, or by sacrifice, as you have seen me. [53]

O Arjuna, only by single-minded devotional service, can I be understood in this universal form. Only in this way can you see and enter into my eternal form. [54]

> *O Arjuna, those who act in My name, considers Me as the highest goal, is devoted to Me, is free from attachment and feels no ill will towards any creature, they realize Me. [55]*

Note

Some people use Krishna's urging Arjuna to fight to protect a race of people from genocide as their reason or excuse to fight today. Others cite their own religion or God telling them to start war. The fallacy of this issue has been addressed in the Prologue. Here we look to learn from the metaphors of this situation.

Exercise

Think of times when you chose to protect someone or something that was in danger. Perhaps in the line of duty as an officer, fire-person, or soldier; or maybe at work, you had to speak up or act to protect civilians or the planet.

Or consider a time you had to make a stand for what you believed, that went against the views of your family and friends.

What was the outcome of your confrontation? Did you find in the end greater self-worth? Did you eventually realize a better way of life, job, or a more peaceful lifestyle?

Vishwaroop: Lord Krishna's universal form

Chapter 12
How to Love God

Arjuna begins by asking,
Of the people who follow the two forms of God-worship (manifest and personal form), which path brings more wisdom/enlightenment?

Some people meditate on the eternal, unmanifest, unbounded abstract God. Others feel drawn to a personal form of God, such as Krishna, Jesus, or Buddha. Arjuna is wondering which is the wiser path to follow.

Krishna says,
Those who worship the form of God are those who know Him best. Eventually, the formless path will bring a person to God; however, it is a more difficult method owing to its unimaginable challenges.

If someone asks you to think of something that cannot be imagined, such as eternal unboundedness, it cannot be done. Even for those who have a sense of eternity, when life gets tough, it is just easier to think of 'someone' to tell your troubles. So it is that people are more naturally drawn to a personal form of God.

Thus, Krishna advises the personal path for the majority of people. He advises people to:

• Surrender all actions to God, since God is the ultimate doer of actions,

• See God as the ultimate goal of life, and

• Worship God with single-hearted devotion.

For those whose hearts are fixed on God, He comes quickly to save the devotee from the misery caused by illusion of the world-as-reality. Resting one's understanding in God brings one to live in God forever.

Krishna then addresses another common issue, the inability to concentrate on God during meditation.

Those who cannot fix a steady mind on God through mental meditation can instead perform devotional deeds. This can include helping the needy, performing pleasing rituals, and chanting devotional songs (*bhajans* or singing God's praise).

For those who fall through the cracks of the above categories, Krishna says there are some who cannot even practice devotional activities. For them, Krishna recommends devoting their work to God, by saying 'whatever I do is for God.' This is an acceptable form of meditation that brings a person to Self-Realization. And those who do not have even the presence of mind to devote their actions to God should take refuge in God, offering God the results of their actions. If you earn fame or fortune, say that God has done this and that it is God's fame or fortune. So if a person does not think of God prior to action, let them, at the time of result, praise God and offer God all they have gained. [Verse 1–11]

Arjuna said:
Who is considered to have a more perfect realization of You; those devotees who are always single-mindely worshiping You, or those who worship the unmanifest, unbounded? [1]

Lord Krishna said:
Those who focus their minds on Me, worship Me with continuous devotion and full of faith, to My mind they have a better realization of Me. [2]

But those who worship the eternal, unbounded, unknowable, unchangeable, immoveable, impersonal, absolute; having completely controlled their senses through spiritual intelligence, and ever trying to do good for all creatures, they also realize me. [3 - 4]

It is more difficult for those who worship the unmanifest because there is no direct experience of any form. Success is achieved with great difficulty because people identify with the body. [5]

But those who, surrendering all action to Me, attached to Me, meditating on Me with single-minded worshipful yoga; O Arjuna, for these people whose minds are absorbed in Me, I become their savior from the ocean of the birth/death cycle (samsara). [6 - 7]

Focus your mind on Me, with spiritual intelligence for Me; and you shall undoubtedly live in Me always. [8]

> *O Arjuna, if you are able to fully concentrate on Me, then through faithful devotional practice seek to realize Me. [9]*
>
> *If you are unable to practice devotion (in this way), then dedicate your activities to Me. In performing activity in My name you will also achieve perfection. [10]*
>
> *Should you not be able to work in this way, then, taking refuge in Me alone, try surrendering the results of all actions to Me and try to become self-controlled. [11]*

Surrendering the fruits of action is higher than meditation. Peace immediately follows surrender.

Practice means doing, but knowledge means understanding gained from experience; thus, it is more esteemed than action without understanding.

Meditation is a method to go beyond one's reality—to gain greater wisdom of Self and a newer insight into more of who one is. This is more precious than knowledge because knowledge relates to a locked or bound time or place. To know a deeper reality, one must transcend the limits of their belief system and experiences and go beyond the ego-based reality to experience more of one's eternal Soul.

Although meditation allows one to realize a greater self beyond their previously defined self, the actual act of letting go of 'ownership' and 'authorship,' and the giving all to God are actions resulting from surrender. Realization only gives the potential to surrender, that is, it removes the desires that prevent surrender.

Yet, surrendering material life requires real-world action. A person needs to see that they can apply this desireless state to their life. This 'letting go', is the last 'action' a person can do for themselves. Thereafter peace descends on the mind, because the friction is removed when the limits and desires are removed. [Verse 12]

> *Knowledge is superior to practice; meditation is better than knowledge; renouncing the rewards of action is superior to meditation—for from renunciation comes inner peace. [12]*

Krishna describes such a person as one who has no hatred toward any creature, who is friendly, forgiving and compassionate to all. They are free of material and emotional attachment, free from egotism; they are equal-minded in all that comes their way be it pain or pleasure, happiness or sadness, gain or loss. Such a person is content and meditative, self-subjugating, with firm conviction, mind, intellect, and heart dedicated to God. This person is not afflicted by the world and is free from envy, fear, anxiety, and elation. This person is devoted to God and is dear to God.

This person is free from external dependencies, pure of mind and heart, efficient, essential, and unselfish. They who treat all equally (friend or enemy), who behave the same whether being praised or blamed, is a devoted soul and dear to God.

Those who follow this teaching described by Krishna, and who possess strong faith in God as the supreme goal in life, are extremely dear to God; they are supreme devotees (*bhaktas*). [Verse 13–20]

Those who has no envy, but are a friend to all creatures, compassionate with no sense of proprietorship, free from false ego, equal-minded in happiness and distress; forgiving, always content and engaged in determined devotional worship; and whose mind and intelligence are in harmony with Me. They are very dear to Me. [13 -14]

Those who are not disturbed by the world and who never disturb the world, and who are free from elation, envy, fear, and anxiety, they are dear to Me. [15]

Those devotees who are desireless, pure, efficient, free from worry and agitation, and unconcerned with any mundane situation, are very dear to Me. [16]

Those who do not rejoice or hate, grieve or desire, who are impartial to the auspicious and inauspicious; engaged in devotional service, are very dear to Me. [17]

Those people who behave equally to friends and foes, in honor and dishonor, who are impartial in cold and heat, happiness and distress, unattached, equal in praise or shame, contemplative before speaking, satisfied with what comes unasked, unattached to residence, steady-minded, engaged in devotional service, is very dear to Me. [18 - 19]

Those who devotedly live this eternal, nectar-path to Me, full of faith, making Me the supreme goal, are very dear to Me. [20]

Exercises

- In this chapter, Lord Krishna says to think of Him, envision Him, say His name to attain Self-Realization. Some have interpreted this to mean the only way to God is through Krishna. But didn't Jesus also say, 'I am the way'? Doesn't each religion say that God is the way? So if God is eternal-one, then isn't each religion saying the same thing about the same God, only using a different name to label God? Considering the possibility that there really is only one God with many paths to Him (or Her, or It, or nature, spirit, ethics, etc.) does that make your heart open with true love for all humanity, in that we are all related—all children of the same God?

- Consider times when you have been able to let go of trying to make situations work out the way you 'think' they should, and find the result to be something greater than you imagined. What does that experience feel like? From these positive results, does it give you more faith to be able to let go more often in the future?

- Krishna describes qualities of an enlightened person on page 128. Search yourself to see how many of these qualities you have found within—even a few times. Cultivate them. Pray that these highest qualities grow in your life.

- Being content with what comes your way should not be taken to mean that you accept your worst behaviors and their resulting karma visited upon you. Rather consider the idea of 'practicing being content' to mean, doing your best to think, speak, and act using your highest qualities for the good of yourself and others, doing your utmost to always think of God, and offering your actions or the results of your actions to God. Then when you have done your utmost, accept the way life unfolds. Learn the lessons from what unfolds—seeing the best in each situation. All the while, continue cultivating these highest qualities in yourself.

- When trying to live a life that causes no harm, consider the effects on three levels: action, words, and thoughts. It is easiest to not physically harm another. It is more difficult to speak with out harm (eg, gossip, blame, judgement). It is most difficult to think only harmonious thoughts. When you can see that all three levels are free from negativity, only then you can truly say you do not cause harm to any creature. It is a worthy exercise, is it not?

Radha and Krishna express
Bhakti; devotion or Divine love

Chapter 13
How to Distinguish Soul From Body

Arjuna now asks for a clearer distinction between the eternal (*purusha*) and the creation that comes from the eternal (*prakrti*).

Arjuna asks:
How do I distinguish between objective life and the inner Soul? What is the difference between intellectually knowable things and the experience of knowingness (of eternal Soul)?

Lord Krishna begins by saying that the body is the objective field of life (*kshetram*). A wise person who knows about the body is called the knower of the objective field (*kshetrajnam*). God is also called the conscious, knowing Soul (*Kshetrajnaha*) in all bodies (*kshetras*).

Having knowledge of both body and Soul comprises true knowledge, which is a form of awareness. Knowledge of the body is a form of wisdom or awareness. One's wisdom awareness can know the true nature of the body from within the body/mind system. God too is the knower/awareness of Soul in all bodies since our Soul can awaken to its own existence and be aware of itself.

To truly know the body means to understand how it is a part of nature, how it functions within nature, and how it develops. Krishna elucidates the learning from verse 5 on.   [Verse 1–4]

Arjuna said:
O Krishna, I wish to know about nature (prakrti) and individual consciousness (purusha), the field of action [kshtra] and the knower of this field, knowledge and the goal of knowledge. [1]

Lord Krishna said:
O Arjuna, the body is called the field [kshetra] and wise call the knower of field Kshetrajnam. [2]

O Arjuna, know Me to be the conscious Soul in all bodies. To My mind, understanding the knowledge of the body and the Soul is true knowledge. [3]

Briefly hear Me describe the field of activity, its nature, modifications, how it is produced; who is the knower of the field or Soul, and what are its powers. [4]

Field Body

The nature of the body comprises the five elements (ether, air, fire, water, and earth). There also exists ego, intellect, the five senses of knowledge (taste, touch, sight, hearing, smelling), the five organs of action (tongue, hands, feet, genitals, and anus), and the mind. Within the body is also desire, aversion, pleasure, pain, and a combination of these, fortitude, and consciousness.

Wisdom/Knowledge

The wisdom field comprises the following positive qualities: humility; forgiveness; simplicity; service to a spiritual teacher; purity; steadfastness; self-control; not harming others in action, word, or thought; and not being ostentatious.

Renouncing the sense objects and having ego in balance, being aware of the relative (non-eternal) nature of birth, death, old age, disease, and pain; not being attached to the relative life of self, spouse, children, home, fame, fortune, but being attached only to the eternal Soul or God; being equal-minded in the beneficial and nonbeneficial life that comes to you. Having one-pointed or unwavering devotion to God, preference for seclusion, distaste for large groups of people, and realizing the essence of Truth.

Each of these can be intellectually understood at first, but that is insufficient to truly know what they mean. Only by directly experiencing these qualities in one's own life can one then say that they truly know what these qualities mean.

Anything other than what is listed here is to be known as spiritual ignorance. Krishna next tells what is worthy to be known. Knowledge of this brings awakening of eternal Self-Realization.

Eternal God (Brahman) has no beginning or end (it has no boundaries to experience things). It is neither existing (*sat*) nor nonexisting (*asat*). It is said that eternal God has hands and feet, a head, eyes, a mouth and ears everywhere in creation; God exists and envelops everyone.

God is what makes our senses work, yet is independent of, or beyond the senses. He has no qualities or *gunas*; She is propertyless. Yet It experiences the *gunas,* exists inside and outside all beings (eternity has no boundaries and thus has no inside or outside). God is moving and nonmoving; is incomprehensible owing to the lack of boundaries. He is far and near at once; She is everywhere, an unbounded and omnipresent Soul.

Eternal God is indivisible, yet can be seen as divided as humans, animals, or nature. It creates, sustains, and concludes all things in creation. He is the light of all lights (beyond darkness). She is knowledge, the knower, and the goal of knowledge that dwells in all hearts.

This is the summary of the field of knowledge and the knowledge to be known. Krishna says that God's devotees, knowing this, are able to become one with God and merge individual Soul (*Jiva*) with universal Soul (*Paramatma*).

Prakriti (nature) can be said to have no beginning, because it comes from *Purusha* (eternal Soul). Yet in relative life, all of nature has a beginning, middle, and an end. The entire creation is born of the three *gunas*.

Now Krishna clearly discriminates between Prakrti and Purusha:

- Prakrti is responsible for the cause and effect in life.

- The embodied Soul (the person) is the cause of experiencing pleasure and pain.

- *Purusha* (the Soul) experiences the *gunas*; attachment to *gunas* causes rebirth.

- The Soul within the body is the known by many names, including witness, Supreme Self, God, and *Atma*.

The person who knows the Soul and the nature (with its *gunas*) avoids rebirth. That is, when a person realizes that inner self is Soul and body and all things in nature are also Soul, then all that exists is Soul. Soul is eternal—ever existing—so where is birth and death in this complete vision of eternity?

Krishna next says there are many paths to such a full realization:

a) Meditation (*sadhana*)

b) Intellectual wisdom (*jnyan*)

c) Action (*karma*)

d) Those who have little knowledge worship yet have been taught by spiritual guides, they too can attain Self-Realization.

In other places, Krishna also speaks of combinations of these paths as well as *bhakti* (devotion) imbibed in the paths. Whatever is in this creation develops from the eternal and the relative forms of Soul (*prakrti* and *purusha*). As the Soul is in everything, God exists equally in all beings and nature. The wise man sees this through direct experience. They see the same God or Soul within everything, everywhere, and everyone equally. The wise woman sees that it is nature alone that performs all action. The Soul is merely the unacting witness.

The wise see the unique existence of all beings, creatures, and nature as nothing other than Soul. That wise person has attained Brahman or Self-Realization. This is a vision of that which has no beginning or end, with no *gunas* or properties.

A mirror can reflect a rose. The mirror can become dirty or it can be painted, covered, or broken. Although the reflection of the rose changes as the mirror's surface changes, the actual rose is never affected. In this way, action in the world of nature can never touch or affect the actual eternal Soul.

Just as the sun illumines all the earth, the Soul, dwelling within all bodies, illuminates all bodies. The realized people who have this eye of wisdom perceive this distinction between body and Soul and are liberated from the enslaving delusion. [Verse 5–35]

This truth has been sung in various ways by the seers, in the Vedic hymns, in various Brahma Sutra aphorisms with their sound logic and reasoning, and by conclusive evidence. [5]

The great elements (earth, water, fire, air, ether), egotism, intellect, unmanifest nature, the 10 organs of senses and action, mind, and the 5 sense objects (desire, hatred, happiness, sadness, determination); all these comprise the field of activities and interactions with the body. [6 - 7]

Humility, unostentatiousness, non-injury, forgiveness, simplicity, service to Guru, purity, steadfastness, self-control; renunciation of sense-objects, absence of egotism, realization of the evils of birth, death, old age, disease, and pain; non-attachment, non-identification of the Self with children, wife, home and the rest; even-mindedness in pleasant and unpleasant events; single-minded and unwavering devotion to Me, resorting to secluded places, aversion to large gatherings of people; constant devotion to spiritual knowledge, realization of the essence of Truth. This is declared to be wisdom; what is opposed to this is ignorance. [8 – 12]

Now I shall explain that which is to be known, by realizing this, one attains immortality. The known is beginningless and subordinate to Me. It is neither existence nor non-existence. [13]

With hands and feet everywhere, with eyes, heads, and faces everywhere, hearing everything; that reality exists pervading the entire creation. [14]

It is the source of the senses, yet is without senses; unattached, yet sustains all; devoid of qualities (gunas), yet is the master of qualities. [15]

It is within and without in the moving and nonmoving, incomprehensible due to Its subtleness; It is far and near. [16]

Indivisible yet appears as divided among creatures; the creator, sustainer, and preserver of all creatures. [17]

It is the light of illumination and beyond darkness. It is knowledge, the One to be known, and the Goal of knowledge that dwells in the hearts of all. [18]

The field, knowledge, and that which is to be known have briefly been described. My devotee, understanding all this, become one with Me. [19]

Understand that nature (prakrti) and Soul (purusha) are without beginning. Also understand that that all modifications and qualities (gunas) are born of prakrti. [20]

Prakrti is said to be the source of cause and effect, while the embodied Soul is the cause of experiencing pleasure and pain. [21]

The Soul experiences the qualities (gunas) born of nature (prakrti). Attachment to the qualities causes birth in good or evil wombs. [22]

The supreme Soul in the body is called the 'witness', the sanctioner, a sustainer, the experiencer, the Ultimate controller, and the Supreme Self. [23]

Those who understand the Soul, nature, and the qualities, however they are living, are not born again. [24]

Some, through meditation, realize the Soul by the Self within themselves; others through wisdom; and yet others through the path of action. [25]

Still others, not having much knowledge, worship as they have heard from other (wise souls); even they surpass death through faithfully following what they have heard. [26]

O Arjuna, whatever is born, whether animate or inanimate, know it is produced from the interaction between the field of activity and the knower of the field of activity. [27]

Anyone who realizes the eternal consciousness within all living things everywhere, and is imperishable within these perishable things, realizes the Truth. [28]

Those who see the Supreme God equally everywhere, they do not hurt the Self by the Self, therefore, realize that supreme goal. [29]

Those who see all actions are performed by nature (prakrti) only, and the Self is not acting, see the Truth. [30]

Those who see the separateness of beings are situated in the Universal Soul, and they grow from that oneness alone, then they fully realize the Ultimate Truth (Brahma). [31]

O Arjuna, without beginning or qualities, the Supreme Soul is unchangeable. Though it lives in the body, it neither acts nor is affected by actions. [32]

Just as all-pervading ether is never influenced, so the Eternal Soul is all-pervading yet is never influenced. [33]

O Arjuna, just as one sun illuminates the entire word, so the eternal Soul dwelling in bodies illuminate all bodies. [34]

With the eyes of wisdom, those who see the distinction between the body and Soul, and the liberation from nature, attain eternal Self-Realization. [35]

Exercises

- Have you ever experienced the state of 'witnessing'? Maybe you were playing ball, or acting, or speaking; maybe you were reading, listening to music, or absorbing nature. Suddenly you realize that things are going on by themselves and it is as if you are watching a movie or a play. You may see yourself swinging a bat, or talking to a group of people, but you realize it is all going on without you thinking about what to say or do. This experience is a glimpse of witnessing. Also note, if this is not an experience you had, it is of no real importance. It is only discussed here to give an example of the witnessing state.

- Think back over the course of your life; when you were a child, a teenager, a young adult, a senior citizen. Over this span of time you will notice many things changed in your life; your feelings changed, your beliefs and perspectives changed, your body is always changing. Still, with all this change, you are basically 'you'. Something about you remains the same. Reflect on this non-changing 'you' to become more aware of your non-changing Soul.

- It is interesting to consider what is eternal and what has time limits. When we are young, we think we will live forever (we may not even *think* about it). As an adult we may group things into non-changing or everlasting categories—trees, mountains, oceans, and other places in nature. In reality, these things are always changing too. If we could step back and see one thousand years into the future, we would see the trees have died, mountains and waterways changed form, and even societal ideas and norms that were 'absolutely believed' in our day have made way for new views. Contemplating what is truly eternal helps give perspective on what is of value in this life. The longer things last, the more value they have. Kindness, love, and gratitude are some values that help awaken one's awareness to their eternal Soul. Trees, mountains, and waterways have existed a long time and we derive benefit from communing with nature. Take time to discover the lasting values within you; appreciate and cultivate them. Incorporate these things into your life evermore.

When caught up in a hectic lifestyle, take some time to analyze the things you are doing; the things you are chasing after, the things you feel you 'have to buy' and 'have to do'. Are they of lasting value? Will they give you the same peace and sanity you are longing for? If not, then you can choose to stop those short-term actions and replace them with more long-term choices. Just because 'they' say this is the way to do things, doesn't make it right for your best interests. Think for yourself, test things out to see if they really work to your long-term advantage. In this way you can take control of creating a more peaceful, harmonious life for you and your family.

Discovering one's Soul in the core of the body

Chapter 14
The Yoga of Guna Distinctions

Krishna continues his talk about distinctions, however, he shifts his focus specifically on the *gunas* (nature's properties of creation, sustaining, and dissolution). Again, Krishna says after attaining supreme wisdom through experience, a person no longer needs to be reborn.

Nature (*prakrti*) is God's womb. God places the seed of creation in this womb, and the birth of all beings arise. It is the three *gunas*, *sattwa*, *rajas*, and *tamas*, who are themselves born of nature, who bind the eternal Soul in the body.

Sattwa—with the qualities of being transparent, luminous, and free from negativity—binds the embodied Soul by attachment to the experiences of happiness and knowledge.

Rajas—with the qualities of passion, thirst for pleasure, and attachment itself—binds the embodied Soul through action.

Tamas—with the qualities of ignorance, lethargy, and delusion—binds the embodied Soul by illusion (covering wisdom), idleness (sloth), and sleep.

At various times, each *guna* will dominate one's awareness. When the light of understanding radiates from the person, it is *sattwa* that predominates. When greed, hyper or excessive activity, enterprise, restlessness, or longing prevail, *rajas* prevails. And *tamas* outweighs when behaviors of darkness, inertia, illusion, and delusion are expressed.

A person's future life will depend on the predominating *guna* at the time of death. Dying with the guidance of *sattwa* causes the person to attain a stainless region in the afterlife, where the highest knowers reside. If one dies during a predominately *rajasic* time, they will be reborn to a family and life of excess action. When death comes while a person is ruled by *tamas*, they will be born to dull-minded, people lacking the quality of reasoning.

Deeds	Yield	Person Develops	Life Direction
Good	Purity	Wisdom	Rise upward
Passion	Pain	Greed	Remain in the middle
Idle, Dark	Ignorance	Delusion, Ignorance	Descend

When a wise person can see only the *gunas* as the 'doers' or 'actors' of life (i.e., that they are the only cause of action in the world), and simultaneously sees the Soul or God as that which is higher than the *gunas*, that person becomes one with God (Self-Realization). This person is freed from the endless cycle of birth and death as they realize their true immortal Soul.

This means a person who knows (though direct experience) that they are not doing their actions or any actions in the world, and also see God as above and beyond all actions of the *gunas*, they attain Self-Realization. In the *Bhagavad Gita*, this is an intellectual description of a very intimate, loving connection to God. It was apparently necessary to explain things to Arjuna by appealing to his mind.

Arjuna next asks,
How do you tell if a person has attained Self-Realization; what are their personality characteristics; how do they go beyond the three *gunas*?

Krishna answers,
A Self-Realized person neither craves nor hates any of the predominating *gunas*; they accept whatever *guna* is temporarily in charge. Such a person sits like a witness to the activities of the *gunas*, without being shaken by their effects. The Self-Realized person has an even temperament when life brings pain or pleasure; they see a clump of mud and a handful of gold as the same; they act the same while being praised or being condemned. A person who has crossed beyond the three *gunas* will be seen to behave the same, whether being honored or dishonored, acting the same to friends or foes, and giving up selfish endeavors. Such a person serves God with unwavering devotion and attains Oneness with God (*Brahman*). God is the

absolute, eternal *dharma* (righteous life-path), ever steady, absolute bliss.

The term *guna* has been used since the beginning of the book. In this chapter and in the upcoming chapters, there is specific and in-depth focus of the *gunas*. Still, *gunas* seem difficult to grasp from a Western point of view.

The best analogy I can find is that the *gunas* are like a movie projector or a DVD player. Imagine a dark room, where it seems that nothing exists. Then turning on the player, suddenly there is light, sound, and thoughts, ideas, and emotions. Horror movies produce fear in the viewer; thrillers cause tension; drama causes sadness; comedies create happiness.

If a person were to watch TV more than live their life, they would not be able to distinguish between what is real in the world and what is pretend. There are stories of people who have met actors and yelled at them for what their character did on TV or in the movies. They did not realize that the actors were different from the roles they were playing.

So the *gunas* are like the movie projector. This world of objects, sounds, emotions, feelings—all is simply a projection of the three *gunas*. In science fiction movies such as Star Trek, people engage in virtual reality, visiting fictitious places that are seemingly real. Virtual reality is analogous to the *gunas*.

Beyond the *gunas* is the still, eternal nonchanging, ever-blissful Soul or God. This is why the Vedic texts admonish a person to know the source of the *gunas* and to live in that existence even while watching the movie called life that is a product of the *gunas*. Know the nonchanging truth, and the movie will never cause undue suffering. [Verse 1–27]

Lord Krishna said:

I shall again describe the supreme wisdom, the best of all knowledge, knowing which all the sages attained ultimate perfection. [1]

Following this wisdom, attaining my nature, one is neither reborn again during universal creation nor destroyed during universal destruction. [2]

O Arjuna, the entire nature is the womb into which I plant the seed that generates all of life. [3]

O Arjuna, whatever forms are produced from all the wombs, the great nature (prakrti) is the womb and I am the seed-bestowing father. [4]

O mighty-armed one, the qualities of goodness, passion, and ignorance (sattwa, rajas, tamas), produced by nature, enslave the unchangeable, embodied Soul in the body. [5]

O sinless one, of these, purity (sattwa) is transparent, resplendent, and healthy; attaches a person to happiness and attaches them to wisdom. [6]

O Arjuna, know that the quality of passion (rajas) causes desire for sense gratification and enslaves the embodied Soul by attachment to the results of actions. [7]

O Arjuna, understand tamas to develop from ignorance. It deludes all creatures and binds through illusion, lethargy, and sleep. [8]

O Arjuna, sattwa attaches one to happiness, rajas to sense pleasures, and tamas obscures wisdom, to illusion. [9]

O Arjuna, sometimes sattwa rules rajas and tamas, sometimes rajas dominates over sattwa and tamas; and sometimes tamas predominates over sattwa and rajas. [10]

When illuminating wisdom manifests through the bodily senses, know this to mean sattwa prevails. [11]

O Arjuna, when greed, excess action and enterprise for reward, restlessness, and longing are present, rajas rules. [12]

O Arjuna, when darkness, inertia, illusion, and delusion are prevalent, tamas is in control. [13]

When a body transitions to death predominated by sattwa, at that time they attain the highest regions of heaven. [14]

When a body dominated by rajas dies, one is next born among those attached to action. When the body ruled by tamas dies, it is reborn in the animal kingdom. [15]

The return on virtuous actions is declared pure (sattwic). The return on actions based in desire (rajas) is pain. Foolishness is the return on actions based on ignorance (tamas). [16]

Wisdom grows from sattwa; greed from rajas; delusion and ignorance develop from tamas. [17]

Those living sattwa go upward; those living rajas dwell in the middle; and tamasic-living people go downward. [18]

When one sees there is no doer beyond the gunas, and knows the Supreme Lord that is higher than the gunas, then they realize My true nature. [19]

When the embodied being goes beyond the three gunas, from which the body grew, liberation from birth, death, decay, and pain results; attaining immortality. [20]

Arjuna said:
O Lord, what are the signs of one who has gone beyond the three gunas? What are their characteristics, and how do they go beyond the gunas? [21]

Lord Krishna said:
O Arjuna, those who are neither adverse to experiencing illumination (sattwa), excess action (rajas), or delusion (tamas), nor crave them when they disappear; [22]

who sits unconcerned, unmoved by the gunas, remaining firm in the knowledge that the gunas are the only agents of action; [23]

who remains equal in pain and pleasure, and sees a lump of earth, a stone, and gold alike, who wisely is the same in praise and blame; [24]

who remains unchanged in honor and dishonor; treating friend and foe alike; who has given up all selfish undertakings; they are said to have gone beyond the gunas. [25]

Those who, while surpassing the gunas, lovingly and continuously worship Me, realizes the onesness of life (Brahman). [26]

I am the home of Brahman, the unchangeable, immortal, eternal life purpose (dharma), and absolute bliss. [27]

Exercise

- Review the *gunas* as they prevail in your life (happiness/knowledge, hyper/longing, idle/sleep). Notice if they cause your mind and actions to become imbalanced—causing behavior you normally wouldn't express if your ideal self was in charge. If you see an imbalance, do your best to regain balance and merely witness the *guna's* effect.

The 3 Gunas

Sattwic behavior: purity, positivity

Rajasic behavior: anger, excess activity

Tamasic behavior: lethargy, gluttony

Chapter 15
How to Uproot the Cause of Illusion

Krishna begins with a metaphor.

There is a tree called *Peepal* or *Ashwattha*. This is said to be an upside down tree because the branches are its roots and its roots grow upward where branches are normally found. These roots eventually curve downward growing back into the soil, becoming a new part of the tree trunk. In this way it is considered an eternal tree because it keeps growing itself anew.

Ashwattha means, unable to last until tomorrow (*shwah*), denoting impermanence as it is also known as the tree of the senses, creating relative, temporary objects that reside in an upside-down position (ie, the senses think they are real and eternal but in fact they are temporary—not lasting until tomorrow. The leaves of the branches are the Vedic hymns (*dharma* or the universal laws of the universe). The buds on the branches are the *gunas*' sensory-objects. At the roots are the three *gunas* that feed the roots of the tree. The roots stretch down into the world, creating actions among humans. People water the roots of the tree with the actions of the three *gunas*.

The roots are eternal and the fruits on the branches are temporary, ever-changing. This suggests that a wise person sees all of life as ever-changing and temporal. To know the unchanging, eternal life, one must go to the root of life beyond the *gunas*.

This can be seen more clearly in yet another metaphor—an *Ayurvedic* metaphor. One reason *Ayurveda* is such an effective healing system is because it does not dwell solely on ever-changing symptoms: it addresses the root of a health disorder. So, going beyond the disease of ignorance of God, going beyond the emptiness or void of living without full connection to spirit, a person will find greater connection of feeling through meditation, service, intellect, and devotion—a combination of all of these elements—and advance beyond all that is created by the *gunas*. They will then see and feel the eternal loving connection with God.

Imagine people walking around the world, seeing fruit from this tree before them. As they partake of the fruit—without knowledge of the roots up above—they become bound to the results of eating the fruit. Each action (enjoying the objects) leads to repercussions (consequences) that keep the person locked into seeing only the fruits and not the roots or beyond. Only the wiser or enlightened people can see beyond sensory objects.

This *Ashwattha* tree analogy clearly evokes the story of the Garden of Eden, where the fruit of the tree of knowledge was forbidden to be eaten. From the *Ashwattha* analogy, we can say that the fruit of knowledge in the Garden of Eden, parallels knowledge of temporary sense objects. Upon eating such an apple, the mind becomes obscured to the eternal source of the apple—and this is what suffering means in Vedic terms—the banishment from living in the eternal of the full loving connection to God.

We can say that it was not God who banished Adam and Eve from the Garden of Eden, from that loving, full connection or hugging of God. Rather, it was Adam and Eve who, by giving importance to relative and ever-changing life (by seeking knowledge from the apple), made the choice. Their actions brought about change (cause and effect). They themselves caused the severing of emotional ties with God. People are after all ultimately responsible for creating their situations—for better or worse.

The everlasting nature of the tree is invisible to the human eye. The wise cut down this deep-rooted tree by the mighty sword of detachment to the *gunas* and all that the *gunas* develop, including the senses, objects, desires, and ego.

Krishna urges all people to pray to attain that safe haven where there is no return to relative changes that separate the Divine lovers—God and the person. He urges us to stay in the ever-hugging eternal, Divine embrace and participating in the ever-joyful dancing, singing, and praising of the name of God.

Let us live in this world, but be not a part of it. Let God drop the ripe fruit in our lap that will sustain us. Why work for that which, when ripest and sweetest, will automatically fall into our laps. This is what the 'Land of Milk and Honey' signifies: a garden of Eden. This sweet life (*sat-chit-ananda* or eternal bliss) can be lived by all who can see beyond the three *gunas*.

Instead, humans struggle and toil unduly for the ever-changing objects of enjoyment, which, ironically cause them more suffering and misery. It is like a drug addict who, when not high, suffers through withdrawal symptoms, and yet, when taking the drugs, becomes enslaved to them. A more subtle form of addiction—choosing temporal pleasure—cuts one off (self-banishment) from their true eternal, Divine birthright.

> *Life is but a stream I go a-fishing*
> *Henry David Thoreau*

Thus, we are advised to live in the world, but not run after the fruits of pleasure; rather, work to locate the very beginnings of the roots and cut asunder at their source. Only then can a person live on this earth as it is in heaven: one with God, on earth and eternally as Soul-spirit.

The people who can see the tree as it truly functions, who have uprooted the *gunas* and realized the eternal beyond the *gunas*, they attain nonattachment, ever attuned, ever united with God. Their attachment to passion has ended, free from conceit, devoted to spiritual knowledge, desireless from personal wants, freed from the opposites (pleasure or pain, happiness or sadness, wealth or poverty, beauty or ugliness, and so on). No longer deluded, arriving at God's eternal home, a person never returns to the empty waif-like state of anguished separation.

God's eternal home cannot be seen by the light of the sun or moon, or by fire. That part of the individual eternal Soul (*Jiva*) attracts the mind and five senses living in nature (*prakrti*) to the more appealing eternal love of God. [Verse 1–7]

Lord Krishna said:
The Ashwatta [Peepal] tree has it roots above and branches below, and is used as a metaphor for eternal life. The Vedas are the leaves of the tree. Those who understand this understand the Vedas. [1]

> *The tree branches extend downward and upward, nourished by the gunas; its sprouts symbolizing sense objects. Its roots stretch down below in the world of humans, creating actions and reactions. [2]*
>
> *The real form of this tree cannot be seen in this world; its beginning and origin, too, cannot be understood. But with determination one must sever this strongly rooted Peepal tree by the mighty sword of non-attachment; thereafter, seek the place, after which having gone, one never returns. There, surrender to the Supreme One from whom everything eternally begins and in whom everything lives. [3 - 4]*
>
> *Free from ego, illusion, and false attachments, understanding the eternal and transitory, free from lust, liberated from dualities like pleasure and pain, the wise reach the shelter of the eternal kingdom. [5]*
>
> *The sun does not illumine that place, nor the moon, nor fire. Those who reach it never return; that is My supreme abode. [6]*
>
> *The living creatures in this world are My eternal parts. They draw out the senses and mind. [7]*

When a person's individual Soul (*jiva*) leaves a body at death and they take on a new body (reincarnation), their mind, their five senses, and their intuition travel with the Soul, just as the wind carries a flower's aroma across the land. As the Soul settles in the new body, it begins to use the five sense organs, intuition, and mind in that new body to experience the life.

The *gunas* delude the untrained person from seeing their Soul, leaving them only to experience transitory objects and pleasures through the senses. Only the wise can see past the *gunas*; the undevoted or insincere cannot perceive God who is beyond the three *gunas*.

Krishna says that all light—be it from the sun, moon, or fire—is, in essence, the light of God. God penetrates all objects in creation, including the sun, moon and fire—the nurturer of all, the life sap that nourishes the herbs and foods. As fire resides in trees, God resides in the human body, united with *prana* (inhalation) and *apana* (exhalation) to digest the four kinds of food. (Foods are categorized by the different methods of required to bring them into the body: chewing, sucking, licking, or drinking).

Krishna says,

God sits in the hearts of all. From God comes memory, wisdom, intellect, as well as their loss over time. God is the author and knower of the Vedas. God is that which appears in the Vedas. [Verse 8–15]

When the Soul moves from body to body, it takes the senses and mind as the air carries aromas. [8]

The embodied Soul governs the ear, eye, sense of touch, taste, smell, and the mind. Thus enjoying sensory experiences. [9]

The foolish do not understand how a living Soul can leave the body, nor can they grasp what sort of body they enjoy due to the actions of the gunas. But those whose eyes are trained in this wisdom can understand this. [10]

Those practicing yoga and who are Self-Realized, can see this clearly. But those who are not Self-Realized, even though trying, cannot see what is occurring. [11]

The radiance that emanates from the Sun, Moon, fire, and from the entire universe, is from Me. [12]

Permeating the planets, I support all by My energy (ojas). I become the soma (eternal moon nectar), and thus supply the essence to all plant life. [13]

I am digestive fire in every body; I am the inhalation (prana) and the downward air (apana), through which I digest four kinds of foods (masticate, suck, lick, drink). [14]

I am seated in every heart; from me comes memory, wisdom, and forgetfulness. I am that which is known in the Vedas. I am the compiler of Vedanta and the knower of the Vedas. [15]

There are two beings in the world (perishable and imperishable). All beings are perishable, but their Soul never perishes. Beyond this, there is the highest being, the Supreme Soul (*Paramatma* or *Purushottam*) who pervades the three worlds and supports these worlds. God is even beyond the imperishable world.

The wise who know God as *Purushottam* know all and worship God with wholehearted devotion.

Krishna says that this is the most profound teaching. Understanding this (that is, experiencing it) one attains Self-Realization and has fulfilled their life's purpose and mission. [Verse 16–20]

There are two kinds of beings in this world, perishable and imperishable. All material things are perishable, and all spiritual things are imperishable. [16]

Beyond these, there is the greatest being, the Supreme Lord, pervading the three worlds and supporting them. [17]

As I am beyond the perishable and above the imperishable, in the world and in the Vedas and I am praised as the Supreme Being. [18]

O Arjuna, those who are free from delusion, knowing Me as the Supreme Being, understanding all, fully worship Me with devotional service. [19]

O Arjuna, this is the most profound teaching, knowing this, one attains Self-Realization and fulfills all duties. [20]

Exercise

- Review your most troubling or stress-producing life issues. Look beyond the actual trouble and search their root cause. Try to find and amend the thoughts and actions that are causing the resulting stress.

Peepal tree; its roots grow down from the top and reaching into the earth to form new parts of the trunk

Chapter 16
How to Manage Divine & Demonic Traits

The discussion of Divine and demonic personality traits will best be viewed as a tool for self-improvement rather than as a way to judge others. This will be discussed in more detail later in the chapter.

Lord Krishna lists the Divine qualities as:

Fearlessness	Non-harming	Vigor
Pure hearted	Truthfulness	Forgiveness
Scripture study	Lacking anger	Fortitude
Charitable	Renunciation	Purity
Sense control	Peace	Not hateful
Sacrifice	Not slander	Not prideful
Modest	Compassion	Not fickle
Austerity	Not coveting	Simplicity
Gentle	Steadfast in spiritual union	

Lord Krishna lists 'demonic' qualities as:

Ostentatious	Conceited	Cruel
Arrogant	Angry	Ignorant
Deluded	Impure	Poor conduct
Untruth	Vain	Hypocritical
Prideful	Lustful	Miserly
Greedy	Egotistic	Insolent
Unable to tell right from wrong		

Divine qualities lead to liberation, while demonic qualities cause further bondage. The word demonic may be difficult to comprehend and may be substituted with the words cruel or wicked.

One of the demonic qualities discussed by Krishna [Verse 7–8] is a lack of belief in God as creator. Yet it would be a mistake to translate this literally as meaning that all atheists or agnostics are demonic in nature. Rather, it is whether a person has a predominance of nurturing or harsh qualities that defines the behavior. There are many people who don't believe in God because they see the hypocritical commercialization in the name of God, or see people, businesses, or governments using God's name and then bilk people out of money, land, or rights. Others do not believe in a God who has human characteristics. Still others have their own reasons. Rather than 'live a lie in a religion', these people choose to live in what they feel is honest truth. Their motives are pure and good. They too can easily realize more of who they really are (God, Soul, or nature).

Krishna says that people with demonic qualities are enemies of the world, bent on its destruction. They have insatiable desires [Verse 1–10]

Lord Krishna said:
Fearlessness, purity of heart, cultivating spiritual wisdom, charity, self-control, sacrifice, studying the Vedas, austerity and simplicity; [1]

Non-violence, truthfulness, freedom from anger, renunciation, peace, aversion to fault-finding, compassion, non-covetousness, gentleness, modesty, and absence of fickleness; [2]

Vigor, forgiveness, fortitude, purity, freedom from envy and pride; O Arjuna, these qualities belong to people endowed with divine nature. [3]

O Arjuna, pretentious pride, arrogance, conceit, anger, cruelty, and ignorance are qualities belonging to those born with demonic nature. [4]

The divine qualities are conducive for liberation, while the demonic qualities cause bondage. Do not worry O Arjuna, you are born with divine qualities. [5]

O Arjuna, in this world there are two kinds of creatures. One is divine, the other, demonic. I have already explained the divine at length. Now hear from Me the demonic qualities. [6]

The demonic people do not know what actions are in their best interest and in their worst interest. There is never purity or good conduct, or truth in them. [7]

They say this universe is unreal, without creator, without a controller, without cause, originating from mutual union due to lust; no more than this. [8]

Holding this view, the demonic, deficient in spiritual wisdom, having lost connection with their Soul, engage in unbeneficial and horrible action to destroy the world. [9]

Addicted to insatiable lusts, possessed with hypocrisy, pride, and irrational arrogance, out of illusion are sworn to work for impermanent, impure things. [10]

They think sensual enjoyment is the highest feeling, exhibiting baseless hopefulness and hoarding wealth through unjust means. They feel a false sense of grandeur; they believe they are all-powerful and superior others. These people perform sacrifices in name only and not in a positive spirit. They hate God within themselves and all others. These people could be said to have cruel or demonic possession. Yet, there are many leaders, rulers, and dictators who fit this description and they sometimes feel they are doing God's work. However, they often do not lead the lives they profess to believe in. There are countless examples of rulers proclaiming a strict spiritual life, abstaining from worldly things such as alcohol, television, techno gadgets, physical relations, and wealth, but who are heavily involved in one or more of these self-proclaimed vices. It is often difficult to walk the straight and narrow when one has power. As the saying goes,

Power corrupts, and absolute power corrupts absolutely.

According to the Vedic view, the result of such cruel behavior is that the wicked person falls into hell (or various degrees of hell), depending on how cruel they were in life. God sends these people back into the cycle of birth and death over and over into *asura* (godless) families. From this delusional state, they continue to fall ever downward. [Verse 11–20]

They are beset with a life full of unlimited fears and worries; believing sense gratification to be the highest goal of life. [11]

Bound by thousands of desires, overcome by lust and anger, they strive to gain wealth illicitly to gratify their senses. [12]

'This I've gained today, and this I desire to get tomorrow, this is mine, and this wealth will also be mine.' [13]

'This enemy I've killed, others I will also slay. I am in charge, the enjoyer, I am perfect, powerful, and happy.' [14]

'I am rich and aristocratic, who is equal to me? I shall perform sacrifice, I shall give, I shall rejoice.' Thus the demonic are deluded by ignorance. [15]

Afflicted with countless fears and anxieties, enveloped in a web of illusions, addicted to sense-gratification, they fall into a terrible hell. [16]

Self-glorifying, impudent, vain, and haughty due to wealth, the demonic perform sacrifices out of pride, in name only are such hypocritical sacrifices done disregarding scriptural injunctions. [17]

Possessed of self-conceit, power, disrespect, lust, and anger, the demonic hate Me, who resides in their own bodies. [18]

I hurl these envious, cruel, evil, lowest of people into the cycle of birth and death in the wombs of the demonic. [19]

O Arjuna, entering into the demonic womb, birth after birth, unable to attain me, these deluded ones fall to lower states. [20]

Lust, anger, and greed are the three Soul-destroying gates of hell. Thus, these three qualities are to be avoided as best as possible. A person who is free from these three dark gates, and who tries to develop their Divine qualities, will find their eternal loving God. So scriptures can help inspire a person to develop their Divine (ideal) behavior. With this understanding of ethical behavior, a person is to apply these principles in their daily life. [Verse 21–24]

Lust, anger, and greed are the three Soul-destroying gates of hell. Thus people should forsake these three. [21]

O Arjuna, a person freed from these three gates of ignorance follows what is beneficial for their Soul, thus realize the supreme goal. [22]

Those who ignore the Vedic injunctions, impulsively chase desires. They do not attain perfection, happiness, or the highest goal. [23]

Therefore, let the Vedic injunctions be you authority in determining what is beneficial to do and not do. Learning these Vedic rules of nature, you should live your responsible life in this world. [24]

Contemplation

Now if a person's mind is clouded, they will read into the scriptures whatever desires they wish to validate. So Krishna here is really saying, use your common sense and follow the Divine characteristics. Do no harm, be compassionate, and bless all. Anything less is against scriptural ethics.

In Chapter 2 (Verse 62–63), Krishna explained how much trouble anger can cause. Attachment to objects causes longing for the object, and unfulfilled desires causes anger. From anger comes delusion, which births the loss of memory, which in turn ruins discrimination (the topic of this chapter). With the loss of discrimination a person perishes.

In Chapter 3 (Verse 37), Krishna said that desire is anger; it is born from *rajas guna*. It is a craving that can never be satisfied, thus causing a person the greatest danger for they can never find peace or Divine love. Anger is the foe in this world.

It is important to distinguish the demonic nature of others and within ourselves. It is always easier to see the faults in others and to see ourselves as being better than others. We see this when different religions kill in the name of God and when governments use demonic actions and justify them because they are dealing with so-called monsters. A sad irony is that both sides in a war see the other side as using demonic methods (torture, chemical weapons, and so on).

So it is virtually impossible to judge another person without becoming 'holier than thou'. At best, we can choose to avoid being around people who behave in a cruel manner, but we are better off not judging that person. When we see a fault in another, it is a sign that that fault is still present in us; otherwise, how could we recognize it?

From this point, it seems that it is more likely that Krishna is speaking about our own inner characteristics. Each person has positive and less flattering qualities. The key is to nurture the favorable qualities and not give any light of day to the darker qualities so they will wither away.

In this way, Krishna provides us with a radar map, turning our discrimination inward towards ongoing self-improvement 24/7. It is like a personal antivirus/spyware software program that we keep running all the time to monitor any untoward behaviors we might exhibit. Just as different websites can expose your personal computer to different viruses, cookies, adware, spyware, and so on, so too can different domains of life incite various qualities that cause us to display anger, impatience, or greed and thus are not in our best Divine interest.

This can also be thought of as a computer game, where the goal is to collect Divine personality-trait power pills that allow the player to jump to higher levels and grow their hearts and minds. Each obstacle teaches us how to react with Divine qualities and avoid using the demonic qualities. Instead of fighting monsters, it is the players themselves who become more Divine or more demonic based on the computer's virtual experience model.

A sincere person, realizing the value and power of self-regulation will gladly turn their attention inward and not look to find fault in another person. There is a saying,

> *People who live in glass houses should not throw stones*

and another

> *Doctor, heal thyself.*

While a similar scriptural saying is

> *Judge not, lest ye shall be judged*

All these maxims relate to the admonition of Lord Krishna that we must work on ourselves to become better people day by day, hour by hour, minute by minute, and second by second—always living in the present. It is a gift that allows us to never become bored, because there is always something we can do to improve ourselves, always some more Divine experience we can open ourselves up to, and always some greater Divine bliss we can feel, live, and be grateful for.

Positive transformation can come from something as simple as learning to play a music instrument, organic gardening, or learning that you always wanted to learn but never found the time until now. Finding ways to express your inner joyful God-gifts relates to simple, mundane, natural pastimes. It also is developed through meditation, and service to others and the environment.

Disharmonious thoughts are like critters in a video game that pop their heads up out of holes in the ground. Prayer for harmonious thoughts to predominate is like a person stepping to avoid the holes, and choosing to stand in a place where they will be safe. So it is in one's best interest to pray to be the best person possible. Pray 'Thy will be done' (not my will); pray to make this the best day possible, letting God determine what is 'best' for us at any given moment. Have no agenda, no outward goal other than to do the best you can with the day God unfolds for you.

When you feel trapped, cry out to God: help me, I am stuck, I am trapped, I am angry, please release me from this; let me come back to your beloved lap. Such sincere and innocent (non ego) behavior quickly reaches God's ears.

Sometimes, however, an answer does not come. At those times, it is helpful to admit you are stuck experiencing your discordant trait and praying to know what you are to learn from the situation.

So we have seen Krishna clarifying the distinction between Divine and demonic personality traits. And we have discussed briefly how to keep working in the direction of developing the Divine traits and how to untie oneself from the demonic qualities through prayer.

Exercise

- Ego has two sides—over praising and denigrating. One says, 'I'm better than the rest', and the other says, 'I'm worse than the rest. Both keep the ego in charge, preventing the acknowledge-ment and growth of one's divine characteristics.

- In a non-judgemental way, review your harmonious and less-than-flattering qualities. Do what you can to nurture the divine qualities, and give no energy or merit to the remaining qualities. This will help develop a more meaningful vision for your life.

God is like anti-virus/spyware—protecting our
positive thoughts from negative ones.

Chapter 17
Understanding the Three Forms of Faith

Arjuna asks Krishna,

What happens to people who disregard the advice of living good, virtuous lives and ignore scriptural injunctions?

Krishna discusses the various dimensions of faith. There are three types of faith that are inherent in a person at birth: *sattwa* (goodness), *rajas* (passionate), and *tamas* (lethargy or dullness). A person's faith is based on their inherent nature; one's faith defines the person. The person and their faith are one. The pure worship the gods, the passionate worship the demons, and the dull worship ghosts. [Verse 1–3]

> Arjuna said;
> O Krishna, those who transgress Vedic injunctions and perform sacrifices from their own imagination, what is their future? Is it sattwa, rajas, or tamas? [1]
>
> Lord Krishna said:
> There are 3 types of faith dependent on one's past life actions; goodness, passion, and ignorance. Now hear about this. [2]
>
> O Arjuna, the faith of each is a result of their inherent nature. People consist of their faith; they are their faith. [3]

Krishna dispels the myth that extreme austerities are somehow a sign of true faith. He says people practicing severe austerities not advised by the scriptures are hypocritical and egotistical; they are moved by lust and attachment, pretentious and arrogant behavior. Such harsh austerities amount to nothing more than senseless torture, and as such, torturing the organs and senses of God. These people are said to have demonic personality.

Foods also have three forms that are liked by each of the three faithful.

- *Sattwic* foods—life-force-increasing foods, bringing energy, strength, health, joy, and cheerfulness; savory, soothing, and pleasing (within limits, Ayurveda says food must be tasty to be healthy, but flavors that overload the taste buds and senses becomes *rajasic)*.

• *Rajasic* foods—bitter, sour, salty, overly hot, pungent, dry, burning; causing pain, grief, and disease

• *Tamasic* foods—stale, putrid, cooked overnight, unclean, lacking flavor, zest, or taste [Verse 4–10]

People of purity worship the demigods; the passionate worship the demons, and the ignorant worship ghosts and spirits. [4]

People practice severe austerities not enjoined by the Vedas out of hypocrisy, egotism, lust, and attachment. [5]

They torture their sense organs senseless. Existing in their body, I know them to be demonic. [6]

Foods are also of 3 types according to the 3 gunas. So too there are 3 types of sacrifices, austerities, and charity. Here are the distinctions. [7]

Foods that increase life-force, energy, health, cheerfulness, and satisfaction, which are succulent, soothing, nourishing, pleasing to the heart, are favored by sattwic people. [8]

Foods that are bitter, salty, overly hot, pungent, dry, burning, and cause pain, grief and disease are liked by rajasic-natured people. [9]

Foods that are stale, tasteless, cooked overnight/putrid, decomposed, foul, and unclean, and other's leftovers are preferred by the tamasic-natured. [10]

Sacrifice, austerity and charitable gifts also have their own three forms of faith.

• *Sattwic* sacrifice occurs when a person does good deeds without desiring any recognition or getting something in return for the good act. Helping others is its own reward. Sacrifice out of a sense of duty is *sattwic*, too, as in the service of a soldier.

• *Rajasic* sacrifice occurs when a person expects something in return for doing a good deed, or they make a showy act of their sacrifice.

• *Tamasic* sacrifice occurs when deeds are done that do not really help the truly needy (an example of helping the needy is giving food to the hungry), or is not done in the spirit of faith and good will.

Krishna then clarifies misconceptions about austerity that are misinterpreted even today. We often hear of people fasting for months, or holding a hand in the air, or burying themselves in sand up to their neck as an austerity. Here Krishna clarifies what helpful austerities are. All else falls under the category of non-spiritual austerity. The three beneficial austerities include those involving the body, speech, and mind:

Austerity of the body involves worshiping positive spirituality (God), showing kindness, spending time around wise, pure, simple people, behaving with self-restraint, purity, and not injuring others.

Austerity of speech involves speech that causes no harm to others, speaking truthfully, saying what you mean, and meaning what you say.

Austerity of thought involves cheerfulness, kindliness, silence, self-control, pure-heartedness, Divine joy, and gratitude, and regularly studying scriptures.

• *Sattwic* austerity is practiced by those who practice three-fold austerity with devotion, resolve, and faith and without wishing for anything in return. Austerity arising out of a sense of duty is also *sattwic*.

• *Rajasic* austerity is practiced when these austerities are performed with the aim to become famous, wealthy, desiring to be worshiped or applauded, or when an austerity is done with an ostentatious and obvious display.

• *Tamasic* austerity is practiced with the aim of deluding or confusing people and hurting oneself or others. [Verse 11–17]

Sattwic sacrifice is performed with no desire for reward, as enjoined by the Vedas; mind focuses only on the sacrifice for its own sake. [11]

O Arjuna, sacrifice performed with a desire for rewards and to show off, is a rajasic sacrifice. [12]

Sacrifice performed contrary to Vedic injunction, without distributing food, and without sacred texts, charitable gifts, and faith is a tamasic sacrifice. [13]

Austerity of the body involves worshiping the Supreme Lord, the brahmanas, the guru, and the wise. Other austerities include cleanliness, simplicity, celibacy, and nonviolence. [14]

Austerity of speech involves speaking truthfully, beneficially and causes no harm to others. Regular study of Vedas is also an austerity of speech. [15]

Austerity of mind involves cheerfulness, compassion, gravity, self-control, and purity of heart. [16]

When this threefold austerity is practiced by devoted, faithful people, not desiring rewards, it is designated as sattwic austerity. [17]

A gift that is given without expecting something in return is a *sattwic* gift. So helping another person, giving charitable gifts, and favors should all be done with the feeling that the giving is the reward itself: *'I am grateful to be allowed to be giving.'*

When a person helps, or gives conditionally, i.e., I'll help you if you help me—I'll do you a favor if you do me a favor; I'll buy from your company if you buy from mine; I'll refer clients to you if you refer clients to me; I'll donate to your campaign if you pass laws to help my company; or, if giving is done reluctantly, or done with the aim to control or manipulate the receiver, these are *rajasic* gifts.

Giving gifts at the wrong time or place, to those who don't truly need help, giving with disrespect or contempt, are *tamasic* forms of giving. It is said that gift-giving carries much responsibility to determine where your money is truly going. You can give to a charity that spends too much of its money on administrative expenses or advertising, or find a charity that keeps expenses to a minimum and uses the majority of the donations for the intended needy. Even if a person gives with good intentions, if the receiver misuses the gift, this is said to be giving a gift to a wrong person. [Verse 18 - 22]

Austerities performed for show, to gain respect, honor, adulation or reward, are unstable and impermanent; they are rajasic austerities. [18]

Tamasic austerities are those performed with delusion, self-torture, or to harm others. [19]

> *Sattwic charity is that which is given for its own sake, without desiring anything in return, in a proper place, time, and to a person who will use the money properly. [20]*
>
> *Rajasic charity is given with the desire to get something in return, desiring some result, or given reluctantly. [21]*
>
> *Tamasic charity is given with disrespect and scorn, at an inappropriate time and place, to one who will misuse the charity. [22]*

A traditional method of giving is now discussed. Saying, *'Aum, Tat, Sat'* (*aum* is the first sound of the universe—so it contains all other words within it; *tat* means 'eternal'; *sat* means 'truth or goodness'— so the full translation means, O this is eternal truth for all times in all places). In ancient times, when giving, the giver would say, *'Aum Tat, Sat'*, then give the gift or start their austerity or sacrifice.

In short, helping others—giving of oneself—humbly, with the thought that I am serving God's children, and the help goes to the truly needy, is favorable and beneficial giving.

As we have discussed earlier, God supports the devotee by assuring they have their basic life essentials (food, clothing, shelter), so there is no need to worry about oneself.

Those whose gifts, austerities, or sacrifices lack true faith, are called *'asat'* or unreal. They have no value whatsoever. [Verse 23–28]

> *Aum Tat Sat (that Supreme Truth or eternal vibration) is said to be the triple representation indicating the ultimate truth. In ancient times the brahmanas used to say this when chanting the Vedas and performing sacrifice. [23]*
>
> *Therefore, as enjoined by the Vedas, the followers of the Vedas always begin sacrifice, charity, and austerities by uttering 'Aum'. [24]*
>
> *Those seeking liberation, without desiring (worldly) rewards, say 'Tat' prior to performing sacrifices, austerities and charity. [25]*
>
> *O Arjuna, Sat means reality, goodness, and auspiciousness. [26]*
>
> *Sat means being steadfast in sacrifice, austerity, and charity; it also means performing action to please the Supreme One. [27]*

> *O Arjuna, those sacrifices performed and austerities practiced without faith are called 'Asat'*
> *(unreal). They are useless in this life and in the next. [28]*

Summary

This chapter shows just how extensive is the range of influence of the 3 *gunas* (*sattwa*, *rajas*, and *tamas*). They pervade all of life, including our thoughts, actions, and faith. Krishna explains the distinction between spiritual and harmful austerity, sacrifice, charity, and eating habits.

Exercise

• Review your life to see when and where you exhibited *sattwic* austerities—selfless giving/non-harming in act, word, and thought. Exercise your *sattwic* austerities as often as you can.

Freely giving to others allows your cup to runneth over

Chapter 18
How to Realize the Ultimate Truth

Arjuna next asks Krishna about *sannyas* (devotional focus on the Divine and serving God's children, instead of personal needs) and *tyaga* (relinquishment). Now that Arjuna has some understanding about the spiritual life and how it works, he is curious to learn about its highest or deepest stages.

Krishna defines a *sannyas* as one who no longer desires to do things for self-reward such as fame, fortune, power, ego, or pride. On the most basic level, *sannyas* is the cessation of selfishness. Yet there are subtle levels, gray areas that may not seem selfish from a social standpoint, but are still forms of wanting something in the relative world. So *sannyas* is the state whereby a person's mind chooses to act for the good of others, for no other reason than to relieve mankind's suffering.

Tyaga is when a person no longer holds onto, cares for, or takes any special pleasure in the results of actions However, even when acting selflessly, by the law of nature, good *karma* will come back to the person. When the person is not influenced by even those good -*karma* returns, this is said to be *tyaga* (full relinquishment).

Action or Inaction

Krishna notes there are differing views about the topic of action; some say all action is to be stopped, and others believe that action that is selfless, such as helping the truly needy through charitable acts, austerity, and sacrifice, is worthy of doing. Krishna weighs in on the subject by distinguishing between three types of relinquishment (*tyaga*).

He says, selfless acts of sacrifice, gifts, and austerity are to be performed, as they purify the person. But the value in these acts only comes to those who perform them without desire for reward. (This discussion is an extension of the topic as discussed in Chapter 17.)

1. *Tamasic* relinquishment: either not doing worthy actions or taking care of one's responsibilities or doing them for selfish motives is *Tamasic*, that is, against spiritual development

2. *Rajasic* relinquishment: done to relinquish action out of fear (eg, running away from a responsibility)

3. *Sattwic* relinquishment: performance of worthy duties and responsibilities without care for anything in return, clinging neither to pleasant acts nor avoiding or disdaining unpleasant ones

So the true relinquisher is one who cares not for the consequences of their actions; they just 'do the right thing' and let the chips fall where they may. A modern day example of this is the 'whistle-blower,' one who cannot sit by idly while their company breaks the law and harms people or the environment. They act knowing they might be fired, demoted, or ostracized; yet, they do what they feel will prevent harm.

Another example of *sattwic* relinquishment is the behavior of loving parents. They sometimes have to discipline their children, even though the children may say, 'I hate you' or 'I don't love you.' Their job is to protect their children, even if it means some temporary ban on the child's happiness or restriction of their movements. So parents must be willing to accept whatever response the child gives to the discipline such as anger or withholding love. And if the child tries to bribe the parent with love, the parent, aware of the scheme, ignores the loving praise, and sticks to their guardian duties.

Thus, *sannyas* and *tyaga* have been clarified by Krishna. Whether living as a monk or on a family path, these principles are equally applicable to people in all walks of life. Acting selflessly and without caring about how the results will profit you personally is a truly spiritual action.

For those who do not relinquish action fully, the consequences or reward of the actions have tri-fold results: good, not good, and mixed. The consequences of their actions follow the person (Soul) into death (of the body). But for those who fully relinquish the results of action—that is, let go of the desire for reward or recognition—the result will be Divine. They will be on the higher or quicker path to Self-Realization. [Verse 1–12]

Arjuna said:
O mighty armed, O master of the senses, O slayer of the Keshi demon. I wish to understand the truth about renunciation (sannyas) and relinquishing the rewards of action (tyaga). [1]

Lord Krishna said:
The wise say, giving up the desires for results of activities is called renunciation (sannyas); and the learned say giving up the rewards of action is relinquishment (tyaga). [2]

Some philosophers declare that all actions should be given up as evil; while others say actions of sacrifice, charity, and austerity are never to be given up. [3]

O Arjuna, hear from Me the actual truth regarding renunciation. There are three types of renunciation. [4]

Actions of sacrifice, charity, and austerity are not to be renounced; but must be performed. Sacrifice, charity, and austerity purify the discriminative mind. [5]

However, O Arjuna, these acts are to be done without any expectation of results, but done as duty for its own sake. This is my highest, definitive conclusion. [6]

Renouncing these prescribed actions is not proper, while abandoning them for illusory reasons is called tamasic. [7]

Those who relinquish action out of fear of physical ailments, thinking, 'this is causing pain', enact greedy (rajasic) relinquishment, the spiritual benefits of renunciation are not obtained in this way. [8]

O Arjuna, one's prescribed duty that is performed for its own sake, while renouncing the desire for rewards, is considered a pure (sattwic) form of renunciation. [9]

This renouncer, endowed with goodness (sattwa), who is neither adverse to disagreeable work, nor desirous of enjoyable work, have no doubts about work. [10]

It is not possible for the embodied to renounce all actions. But those that renounce the fruits of action are called true renouncers. [11]

Those who do not renounce attract an admixture of three fruits (desireable, undesireable, and mixed) after death. But this is never so for those who renounce. [12]

Krishna next outlines five factors taken from Vedic *Sankhya* philosophy that are needed for accomplishing action:

1. The field of action (where you perform the action)

2. The body

3. The senses

4. Bodily functions

5. The body's ruling deities

No matter what a person does, says, or thinks, rightly or wrongly, whether helpful or unhelpful, these five factors are involved. To say that the Soul is the doer would be to express an incorrect or delusional view, because the Soul is eternal, unmoving, and wholly uninvolved in action.

Only those who act without ego or agenda ('I am not the doer') and without concern for receiving favorable or unfavorable results, and who acts without being bound by the action in either way will achieve Self-Realization.

There are some issues with this type of talk however. First, since all people have some combination of *gunas*, and the goal of life is to go beyond the *gunas*, one needs to be careful to not judge others according to their perceived predominant *guna*. This sets up a 'holier-than-thou attitude in one's mind that destroys the goodness of one's good acts.

No human being has a life that is 100% pure. Having human characteristics means, even for the greatest saints, they too must be on guard to not get caught in subtle ego traps.

Secondly, merely having the intellectual awareness that one's thoughts are *rajasic* or *tamasic* is not enough to transition to *sattwic* thinking. In fact, being locked into less than *sattwic* thoughts and actions, even though temporary, is an example of bondage.

A person can see themselves trapped, but not be able to release themselves from these thoughts. It is a subtle form of addiction and is related to the addiction to materialism, greed, pride, and power. Thus, just discussing or reading such lofty ideas as set out by Lord Krishna, is not enough to transform one's life or to liberate the subtlest levels of the reader's mind. It is a good start, however, but then the real work, the lifelong work begins.

So when reading such philosophy, it is best to remember that the words are there to guide you. But when the storm comes and the mind becomes locked by anger, greed, pride, lethargy, or other smaller-minded patterns, one can only pray with the greatest of sincerity and desperation for God to release them from this bondage.

As Krishna has said, God is the doer in life. So even when we are attempting to become free from *rajasic* and *tamasic* mental tendencies, it is actually the grace of God that allows for such release. When times become more despondent, it causes a person to more fully and sincerely (often out of sheer desperation) put all their energies and intentions into calling God for their release and asking for salvation from the current storm. Such storms keep the devotee humble in this ongoing life-process.

Therefore, being the ideal *sattwic* person is something to continually strive for, while looking inward instead of outward. (As previously mentioned, the goal is to move beyond *sattwa* to Eternal Soul; but in the context of mental attributes, *sattwa* is the most desirable attribute prior to eternal transcendence.) [Verse 13–17]

O mighty armed, learn from Me the 5 factors that cause the accomplishment of all action, as it is cited in Sankhya philosophy. [13]

The five factors are the body, the ego, the senses, the various and manifold vital forces, and the eternal Soul. [14]

Whatever action a person performs with the body, speech and mind, whether proper or improper, these 5 factors are the cause. [15]

As such, those who ignorantly believe their body is the only doer, are lacking spiritual wisdom and have no realization. [16]

Those who don't have this egotistical belief, whose understanding is not affected by favorable and unfavorable things, even though slaying these people, they neither slay nor are bound by their action. [17]

Next Krishna discusses the nature of action in depth. The are three causes of action:

1. Knowledge

2. Knowable object

3. Knower

And there are three bases of action:

1. The means to act (eg, senses, limbs)

2. The action itself

3. The doer

In addition to knowledge of and desire to act, there must be the ability to act and a person to achieve the action.

There are three kinds of knowledge, action, and doers, according to the three *gunas*:

1. *Sattwic* action: knowledge (seeing) that all beings are eternal and are a part of the One Soul. (In essence, there is no diversity, since we are all the same Soul.)

2. *Rajasic* action: seeing the separateness in all beings (and not the common Soul)

3. *Tamasic* action: seeing and clinging to one single thing as if it were everything and missing its true eternal essence

An example of *rajasic* distinctions is seeing the media portray how two groups are different from one another (eg, red states and blue states; creating dramatically sharp distinctions between sides to allegedly make a story more engaging), or governments who divide groups or religions to conquer both groups. On the human level, fighting with friends or relatives over property or things is *rajasic*.

Tamasic actions include doing anything in a wholly attached manner; never reasoning whether it is valid; unfounded in truth; clinging onto a person, idea, philosophy, herb, drug or anything material, instead of letting go and embracing the eternal spirit or Soul.

Sattwic actions: following one's duties (responsibilities) without attachment, like/dislike, or desire for the rewards of the action. These people do not seek work; rather they take the work that comes to them in the form of responsibility.

This behavior has no sense of I: the person works as a Divine instrument.

Rajasic actions: acting on the desire that fame, fortune, power, or glory will come to you from your actions. This type of action depletes energy. Those who act *rajasically* constantly work, run, develop, create, fix, and so on. This behavior is greedy, passionate, violent, unclean, easily excited by joy or sorrow, success, or failure.

Tamasic actions: when work is done blindly, without forethought as to reasons, ability, consequences (who if anyone benefits or is harmed by the action). This behavior shows itself as undisciplined, vulgar, stubborn, knavish, indecisive, lethargic, procrastinating, arrogant, or dishonest.   [Verse 18–28]

The knowledge, the object of knowledge, and the knower are the threefold cause of action. The senses, the work, and the doer are the threefold basis of action. [18]

Sankhya philosophy declares knowledge, action, and the doer to be threefold, depending on the threefold nature of the gunas. Hear the details. [19]

The One, unchangeable, unending knowledge that is seen in all creatures is pure (sattwic) knowledge. [20]

Knowledge that sees distinction between different creatures is passionate (rajasic) knowledge. [21]

And the knowledge that is restricted to one kind of work as the whole truth, without reason, unfounded on truth, and superficial, is darkness (tamasic). [22]

Actions ordained, performed without desiring the rewards of the action, unattached, without craving or aversion, is purity (sattwic). [23]

Actions performed while desiring the rewards of the action, with egotism, or with much effort, is rajasic. [24]

Actions done under delusion, without considering one's own ability, consequence, loss, and injury is tamasic. [25]

> *Free from attachment, without egotism, endowed with perseverance and enthusiasm, unaffected in success or failure, is one who works with purity (sattwa). [26]*
>
> *Those whose have passions and desires for reward, greed, malicious, impurity, who are easily moved by joy or sorrow, are overly active (rajasic) workers. [27]*
>
> *Those who are unqualified, vulgar, arrogant, deceptive, overbearing, lazy, despondent, and procrastinating, are ignorant (tamasic) workers. [28]*

People often say that the work they did got them off the track, ie, off their spiritual path. They often ask, should I do A or B; should I build my company or spend more time in meditation? But as we see from Krishna's discussion, it is not what you do but how you do it, or more specifically, the spirit of the choice is the key.

A person can work long hours on a project, and it can be *sattwic* or *rajasic*. If the work feels like it is what they were born to do; if it feels like it is their responsibility; if by helping others the person feels humbled and grateful to be allowed to participate in this action, and when the unpleasant aspects of the work are done in the same spirit, then it is *sattwic* work.

However, if a person is working on a project to become rich, famous, or powerful; working to avoid their family or social life, then this is *rajasic* work. It is a very subtle point, but a little focus on the distinction makes a world of difference in how a person lives their life.

While discussing this point, a common question is raised, 'I choose to work to support my family. Is that not *sattwic* action?' This is a most important question. There are two parts to the answer. By working to support others, this is seen as selfless work, ie, you are not working for your own personal gain, but for others. Still, within this context, a person must choose a respectable job, and not merely do anything, even if it is unethical, all in the name of supporting a family.

Doing *tamasic* or *rajasic* work requires self-aggrandizement and involves ego, either because of a lack of self-worth or by seeking self-contentment. When a person realizes they have done some work that was *rajasic* or *tamasic*, often after things fall apart, they sometimes realize the errors in their ways. The tendency is to swing to the other extreme—self-deprecation. One begins to sulk or dwell in guilt or self-pity. Instead of acting from the point of view of being a good person, the person dwells on how bad they have been. The key here is that the person is still stuck in 'I.' Often people wait for punishment or punish themselves or give up on life for some time. Then they swing back to self-aggrandizement and start the cycle all over again.

It is helpful to know that since both are ego-born (ie, *rajasic* and *tamasic*), if a person changes their intent and does something from a *sattwic* point of view (a selfless act), in that instant, things change for the better.

Often one's greatest growth comes after hitting the bottom, when things are darkest. It is only then that a person becomes motivated to make a change. We see this in people who wait for the last minute to do their homework or study for tests. On a larger scale, we see this in government when nothing gets done until a tragic disaster occurs. Or in personal growth, such as when a person becomes 'sick and tired' of being sick and tired, they finally forgo all the mental chatter, fears, and doubts, and just move ahead in uncharted areas of their life.

So one value of *rajasic* and *tamasic* acts is even though they destroy one's plans and result in embarrassment and humiliation, one must go on. In this way, these less than perfect behaviors sometimes act as a catalyst to the *sattwic* way of life. Eventually, a person may come to realize that they do not have to wait for a disaster to make positive changes and can begin to implement positive actions sooner. This shift from waiting until something goes wrong to correct it marks a change for the positive. By respecting oneself enough to say 'I am worth living a Divine life,' one chooses more harmonious options in the direction of the Divine.

Everything in nature is cyclical. Even the *yugas* (eras of life) start with *sat* (purity) and end in *kal* (darkness), then *sat* again resumes.

So too in the natural lives of people, they do good, slip to some degree off their path, and humbled and willing to accept a more harmonious life, return to their path again, cleansed and more open.

If there is some benefit to *rajas* and *tamas* in this instance, it is that they help to purify the ego from thoughts of too much and too little (that I am the greatest/I am the worst): both of these are detrimental. There is no shame then in admitting mistakes (falling off the *sattwic* path). Be aware to not judge others according to how much *sattwa* you feel appears in their life. Also it would be useful not to focus only on one's crown *chakra* (spiritual energy center) and ignore the baser *chakras*; the implication being that the person does not need to work on 'lower evolved' levels, or that if they work solely on the highest level, the foundations will automatically cleanse. This is a pretense or illusion; it is a form of *rajasic* or *tamasic* thought. As the goal of life is to go beyond all three *gunas* (even *sattwa*), it is best to not let the intellect dwell on or make judgments about *gunas* in your life or in other people's lives.

Therefore, it is suggested here to think of the *gunas* in the following manner. Anything that brings a sense of wonder, a feeling of purity, a simpleness of thought, lightness, innocence, a sense of inner joy for no apparent reason, or a feeling of becoming more childlike, is something beneficial to try to develop in one's life.

Anything that makes a person feel that they know something, trying to convince people of why they are right, gathering intellectual information, understanding the difference between things, feeling better than others, feeling too holy to do some sort of unpleasant work, judging, laughing at, blaming, making excuses, or speaking ill about others; all these are signs that a person is off their path of innocent, devotional, tender God-love. This is hardly an exhaustive list, but it is a start, and it covers the essential behaviors.

Now Krishna discusses the distinction of understanding and fortitude:

Three Insights

Sattwic: understanding and knowing

• When to act and when to wait

• Right from wrong action

• Fear and fearlessness

• Bondage and liberation

Rajasic: having a distorted understanding and

• Not knowing when to act and when to wait

• Confusing right from wrong action

• Not understanding the difference between fear and fearlessness

• Not understanding bondage and not seeking liberation

Tamasic: having no understanding and seeing wrong things as right

• Acting when waiting is more appropriate and vice versa

• Continually choosing wrong actions instead of right actions

• Living and making choices based on fear and not knowing fearlessness

• Living in bondage and not seeking liberation

Three Roots

Sattwic: having the ability to control one's thoughts (in *sattwa* or positivity), and thus speech and actions, roots a person in *sattwa*

Rajasic: clinging to duty, righteousness (and self-righteousness), desire, wealth, desiring rewards of actions, roots a person in *rajas*.

Tamasic: excess sleep, fear, grief, despondency, vanity, and self-conceit roots a person in *tamas*.

The notion of righteousness as an undesirable trait may raise some eyebrows. Krishna has already said that acting out of duty is *sattwic*, but here it is seen in the context of an excess, for example, when action is used as an excuse to get what you want. A thought might start pure, but then degrade into a combination of righteousness and personal ambition. This can be seen when people kill in the name of God's love. Woodrow Wilson, the 28th President of the United States (1913-1921) claimed that God told him to become President. However, late in his life he realized that his unyielding grip on achieving his goals resulted from his own personal desires and lack of patience. Some people can sound self-righteous, even when their ideas or methods are wrong. Sounding righteous does not make a person right; it may give what they say a *rajasic* quality.

Three Pleasures

Sattwic happiness: starts out as poison and ends as nectar and is born of the blissful knowledge of the Soul.

Rajasic happiness: arises from sensory contact and starts like nectar but ends as poison.

Tamasic happiness: begins and ends in self-delusion, owing to excessive sleep, lethargy, and false perception.

There is a saying, 'if it sounds too good to be true, it probably is.' Beware of one who offers you 'easy money.' There is no free ride. There is no free lunch. Anything worth having is worth earning. People run after big, easy, fast money; after fame and praise and often end up in a poisoned situation.

When the eyes see lustful things or the taste buds taste overly rich, sweet foods and beverages, though these start as pleasure, they end in poison, that is, in damage, disrepair, and illness.

However, when one's own awareness realizes, if I make some modifications now, things will be better later, this is *sattwa*. For example, knowing your Ayurvedic *dosha* (constitution), and eating foods that balance that *dosha* such as fresh, organic, whole foods might not unduly excite the taste buds (though it will be tasty and wholesome). In time, however, digestion improves and the body has more energy and fewer health problems. And the mind is more at peace. This is a form of *sattwic* pleasure.

Another example is earning money: One can overcharge a person and get an initial larger sum of money. But if the customer has been hurt by paying so much money, they will look elsewhere for a fair deal; somewhere along the line the seller will suffer. On the other hand, if fair fees are set by the seller (and they earn what they need to survive) and the buyer pays what is reasonable for them to continue to survive, there is a natural interdependency, and life becomes more harmonious. Initial self-sacrifice yields *sattwic* pleasure.

If a student wants to do well in school, they must sacrifice parties for study; and in the end achieve their higher pleasure. If an athlete wishes to win at their sport, they must sacrifice hours, days, and years of their life to excel. If a person wishes to feel love, they must give their love away. In short, the more a person sacrifices or gives away worldly (material) things and knowledge and emotions, the more space they have to receive spiritual gifts in return.

All humans, creatures, and all heavenly beings are under the sway of the *gunas*. Only God, the unchanging source of the *gunas*, can free one from their influence. [Verse 29–40]

O Arjuna, now hear Me comprehensively and individually describe the distinction between understanding and fortitude according to the three gunas. [29]

O Arjuna, pure (sattwic) wisdom knows when to act and when to refrain from acting.; it also knows right from wrong action, fear from fearlessness, bondage from liberation. [30]

O Arjuna, distorted (rajasic) wisdom cannot distinguish between righteous and unrighteous, and proper and improper action. [31]

That ignorant wisdom (tamasic) regards unrighteousness as righteousness, and all things contrary to how they really are. [32]

O Arjuna, continuous determination that motivates mental activity, the life breath, and the senses through unwavering practice of yoga, is sattwic willpower. [33]

But that determination by which one clings to duty, desire, and wealth—attached and desiring is rajasic willpower. [34]

O Arjuna, determination by the ignorant who cannot stop dreaming, fearing, grieving, being despondent, and vain, is tamasic willpower. [35]

O Arjuna, now hear from Me about the three kinds of happiness, through which happiness lasts and pain ends. [36]

That which begins like poison, ends like nectar; this is pure (sattwic) happiness born of Self-Realization. [37]

That happiness that is caused by the contact of the senses with objects, and seems like nectar at first, but becomes poison later, is rajasic happiness. [38]

Happiness that starts and ends in self-delusion, arising from sleep, laziness, and illusion is tamasic happiness. [39]

There is no creature in heaven or earth that is free from the three gunas, born of nature (prakrti). [40]

The Caste System Myth

Lord Krishna then dispels another myth. This time he examines the caste system. Although the caste system has become a hegemonic tool of the corrupt and power-hungry to lord over the masses, claiming that they are holier than others, the system was actually meant to be a horizontal system based in innate or God-given qualifications. For example, the largest, strongest people were best suited to be the soldiers; those with a love of prayer were the priests; those with an affinity for the earth were the farmers; and those with have a penchant for serving were the servants.

This system was meant to create a natural interdependency among the groups: each needs the other to make their lives whole. Each person was given innate qualities necessary for the duties they were given. This was more a matter of the natural expression of certain traits:

Brahmins (priests): serenity, self-restraint, discipline, purity, forgiveness (in heart to even those who seek to hurt), directness and decency, knowledge (book learning and direct personal experience), faith in God.

Kshatriyas (soldiers): valor, spiritedness, constancy, resourcefulness, courage, compassion, a giving nature, leadership.

Vaishya (farmers/shopkeepers): ability to work the soil, protect the cows, and have a propensity for agriculture, animal husbandry, and conducting commerce.

Shudra (servants): natural ability and love of serving others and remaining humble at God's feet.

It is for each person to be completely engrossed in their duties to grow to God. By offering the duties as worship to God, a person merges in love with God.

The most fortunate person is the one who makes their life's responsibilities (pleasant or difficult) as one's duty to God. Responsible action saves a person from stress and the agony of spiritual separation. [Note that while using one's God-gifts, difficulties of a different quality, and less harsh difficulties are incurred then when not following one's life purpose. Some, when experiencing the undue or unnatural suffering caused by the latter, falsely believe they must accept life when it is difficult. This merely confuses the two forms of difficult life. To say that God wants me to accept this unnatural suffering is a mistake. Lord Krishna admonishes people to do their best, not to give up, make matters worse, and blame God.]

By following one's life in this way, a person acts from detachment (not desiring good things and not avoiding bad things), and merely witnesses life as it unfolds in front of them. This process develops gradually over time if the will is there to experience a Divine life.

Here, the saying 'the grass is always greener on the other side' is most appropriate. Krishna speaks of this in Chapter 2 as well. It is better to do one's own duty, though imperfect, than to envy another or try to do another's duty. By gradually learning to give up attachment to all things and accepting life as it unfolds (as it relates to one's duties) is *sannyas*. Such a person does not become entrapped by actions and hence, they become liberated: this is grace in action. [Verse 41–49]

O Arjuna, the duties of Brahmanas (priests), Kshatriyas (soldiers), Vaishyas (business people), and Shudras (servants) are divided according to the qualities (gunas) of their own nature. [41]

The nature of Brahmanas are serenity, self-control, austerity, purity, forgiveness, honesty, knowledge, wisdom, and faith. [42]

The nature of Kshatriyas are heroism, energy, determination, skill, no trace of cowardice in battle, generosity, and leadership. [43]

The nature of business people include agriculture, animal husbandry, and trade. Service is the nature of Shudras. [44]

People attain perfection by following their own nature's activities. Now hear how to gain perfection by following your own qualities. [45]

By worshipping God, the source of all beings, all-pervading, humans can attain perfection through performing their own duties. [46]

It is better to practice one's own duties with mistakes, than to perform another's duties perfectly. Those who follow their own nature's activities do not incur sin. [47]

O Arjuna, a person should not renounce the inherent duties with which they were born; even if defective, because all actions are surrounded by evil as fire surrounds smoke. [48]

Those whose understanding is spiritually detached from everything, with controlled mind, without material desires, realize the highest perfection: cessation of reactions through renunciation. [49]

Qualities of a Self-Realized Person

Krishna has clearly laid out different paths to Self-Realization for different people (depending on their innate nature or *gunas*). He now explains the qualities of a Self-Realized person.

They are insightful, understanding, self-disciplined, masters of the senses (not a slave to them); have strong-healthy wills; live to serve others (selfless though not subservient); are not interested in personal gains; and have no likes or dislikes (is without personal aversions or desires). They enjoy solitude, modest diet, and speech, living in a meditative state, and being dispassionate. Such a person is without pride, violence, arrogance, lust, wrath, possession (no sense of 'I' or 'mine'), and is at peace with themselves.

They are serene, neither desiring nor grieving, wholly devoted to God, knowing God, taking refuge in God, surrendering all thoughts and feelings to God, seeing God as the highest goal, ever devoted to God, having God ever-fixed in their hearts and minds.   [Verse 50–58]

O Arjuna, I will summarize how a person achieving perfection of cessation of reactions attains the highest goal of life (Brahman). [50]

Endowed with pure understanding, self-controlled through willpower, renouncing sense objects like hearing and touching, abandoning craving and aversion, staying in secluded locations, eating moderately, controlling body, speech, and mind; always absorbed in meditation, adept at detachment, forsaking egotism, power, pride, lust, anger, and material things; is peaceful; and is without sense of ownership; such a person is qualified for Self-Realization. [51–53]

Becoming one with the Supreme Lord (Brahman), joyous from within the Self, neither grieving nor desiring, equal to all creatures, that person realizes supreme devotion to Me. [54]

Only through devotional service is one able to realize My truth. When one is fully aware of the Supreme Lord, they immediately enter into Me. [55]

Even though constantly performing all action, those who take refuge in Me, realizes the eternal unchanging abode by My grace. [56]

Mentally surrendering all actions to Me, seeing Me as the highest goal, seeking refuge through yoga, always remaining conscious of Me. [57]

Fixing your heart on Me, you will overcome all obstacles by My grace. But if due to egotism you do not hear Me, you will perish. [58]

This is basically a repetition of all that has been stated throughout the *Bhagavad Gita*. Living moderately, modestly, eating Ayurvedic/*sattwic* diet, and serving others with mind and heart fixed on God.

Now Lord Krishna applies the qualities of a saint to Arjuna's current situation. He says, Arjuna, by your saying, "I will not fight," you tell me that your ego overrides your protector/warrior nature. Bound by your own *karma* (pre-determined actions to be lived out in this life) and *gunas* (nature), your duty compels you to fight. So rather than fight against your nature to protect others, devote all of your actions to God, be detached (having no desires or aversions), keep an even, peaceful mind, and act to prevent a genocide. A motiveless life dedicated to God releases one from bondage. In other words, it melts the wall of ego between the person and God; it unites the two Divine lovers (God and you). Nothing in this life is higher. This is the essence of the teaching. [Verse 59–60]

> *If egotism causes you to rationalize a reason to not fight, the decision will be in vain; your own nature will compel you. [59]*
>
> *O Arjuna, due to illusion you are now wishing to not act according to My instruction. But you are compelled by your own nature to act anyway. [60]*

This is a very profound teaching for a very common situation. People often ask, 'should I do this or the other thing?' Here Krishna says that the question itself is born of ego (should I do). Krishna is saying, whatever you do, dedicate all action, thought, speech, and outcomes to God. This removes personal motive from the picture. Act in such a manner that you have nothing personal to gain or lose from a situation. Only then you can act in a saintly manner.

Having a motiveless life does not mean leading a hopeless life. Quite the opposite, it is the strong desire to feel and love God that engenders this state. Moreover, it can be quite difficult and frightening to allow oneself to lead a motiveless life. Our society teaches us not to stand there, but "do something." We also hear that a mind is a terrible thing to waste. So to understand the subtle difference between a motionless, hopeless, motiveless life and a God-based motiveless life is crucial in order to experience this state. It is very difficult even to describe the differences between the two other than to say it is the intent. Unhappiness, emptiness, anger, vindictiveness, and loneliness are the symptoms of an unhealthy, motiveless life. Conversely, hope, positive intentions, feeling or wanting to be closer to God, wishing to help people, trying to not hurt anyone or think bad of anyone, these are signs that the life is spiritually-based and motiveless.

Included in this instruction on how to live and grow to God, Krishna says, not only do not argue with yourself or others about the 'right way' to do things, but also do not even discuss this secret teaching to those who show no such spiritual qualities of sincerity or integrity; avoid such talks with superficial, immature, cynical, doubting individuals. Know when to speak and when not to.

Discussing this highest teaching with those who are truly ready and thirsty for Self-Realization is the highest act of devotion one can perform for God, and makes that person dearest and most beloved to God. [Verse 61–70]

O Arjuna, the Supreme Lord lives in the hearts of all creatures, causing them to revolve like spokes on a wheel. [61]

O Arjuna, surrender in Him fully. By His grace you will attain supreme peace and the eternal abode. [62]

Thus, I have explained this most profound of all secrets to you. Contemplate this fully, then act as you wish. [63]

As you are very dear to Me I shall repeat My most supreme instructions. I speak for your benefit. [64]

Always think of Me and be My devotee. Worship Me and offer obeisance to Me. Thus, you will attain Me. Truly, I promise that you are dear to me. [65]

Giving up all ideas of righteousness (dharma), take refuge in Me alone. I will free you from all sinful reactions; do not despair. [66]

You should never reveal this to anyone devoid of austerity, without devotion, who does not render devotional service, or to one who speaks ill of Me. [67]

> *Those who share this supreme secret with My devotees, attains eternal devotion unto Me and certainly comes to Me. [68]*
>
> *There is no one more dear to Me than this person (who shares this wisdom with My devotees), and there will never be anyone in this world more dear to Me. [69]*
>
> *Those who study this sacred conversation of ours shall be worshipping Me through the sacrifice of wisdom. This is My conviction. [70]*

Those who live by this teaching will know the intimacy of God's love. But it is not just to be studied and practiced without understanding (direct experience), feeling, or compassion. [Verse 71–72]

> *Even if a person merely listens to this with full faith and without malice, they too become liberated and reach the sacred region of those of virtuous deeds. [71]*
>
> *O Arjuna, have you heard this with rapt attention? O Dhananjaya, are your illusions and ignorance now dispelled? [72]*

After hearing this discourse, Arjuna awakens to the truth, the delusion of his mind dispelled. The teller of the story now also notes that he, too, reciting this story continually grows in bliss, growing ever closer to God. [Verse 73–78]

> *Arjuna said:*
> *O Krishna, by your grace, my illusion is dispelled and realization is restored. I am stable and my doubts are cleared. I shall follow your advice. [73]*
>
> *Sanjaya said:*
> *Thus I have heard this wonderful, electrifying conversation between Lord Krishna and Arjuna. [74]*
>
> *By the grace of Vyasa I have heard this supreme secret wisdom of merging individual Soul with universal Soul directly from Lord Krishna. [75]*
>
> *O King, I repeatedly recollect this wonderful and holy conversation between Lord Krishna and Arjuna. I rejoice again and again. [76]*

O King, repeatedly recollecting that most wonderful form of Lord Krishna, I am awestruck, rejoicing again and again. [77]

Wherever Lord Krishna, master of Yoga, is found; wherever Arjuna the bowman is found; there you will find prosperity, victory, exceptional power, and a sound nation. This is my firm conviction. [78]

Afterthoughts

It is commonly held that we struggle in life to reach some goal, some touchdown, and then we will live on 'Easy Street', never again needing to think or discriminate or work or grow. We won, we 'got it'; now we can sit back and coast. Even in many spiritual circles, the notion of Self-Realization comes with its implied belief that once one becomes Self-Realized, they can navigate on auto-pilot, being impervious to loss and able to rest on their holy laurels. Life is not meant to be coasted through with inattentiveness; it is a life of inner and outer *sadhana* (silent meditation and thoughtfully industrious, active meditation that leads to eternal Divine intimacy with God).

The reality is that life is a continuum. Even the Self-Realized saints are ever learning (though it is in higher, non-material realms), ever growing, ever coming closer to God. No one says, I've had enough air today. I'm done breathing; I've had enough joy today, I'll go back to muck and misery. After falling in love with one's spouse, a person does not say, 'I've got enough love now, I can stop loving them now.' So, too, the ongoing, ever-present growing intimacy with God is something that continues to become an ever more intimate experience, it does not make any sense to put such intimacy on auto-robot or ignore it.

As Lord Krishna said above, full devotion to God, dedicating mind, heart, speech, and actions to God is everything; it is all there is. This is the highest teaching. The poet Rumi calls it ecstatic love, where at times, one's idea of self is annihilated or merged with God, and at other times, it yearns for closer intimacy.

Whatever stresses and challenges are in your life, whatever word you use for God, pray to feel the ever-growing spiritual intimacy, and you will feel God helping you along your path. Pray that all you do is for that one God-experience only. Trade all selfish motives, desires, wishes, powers, and knowledge for the immortal nectar of intimate, ecstatic God-love that comes from silent and active sadhana (meditation and service to humanity).

By praying for this with sincerity, a person will gradually feel the very real, experiential, ever-growing graceful, eternal jubilant love with their personal God.

I pray that all who read the story of the *Bhagavad Gita* and this commentary will take this Divine suggestion to heart. Whatever your religion or spiritual predilection, aim for Divine love in every moment of every day, in every pore of your being, in everything you see, hear, taste, smell, and touch.

Exercises

- Think of times when stress or obstacles were paramount in your life. If possible, examine your thought processes leading up to the event. What choices did you make? Did you have an option to wait, but chose to act, or vice versa? By examining and exercising the decision/waiting process in your mind you become more aware of your choices and their consequences, and subsequently will find yourself making more decisions that lead to more fulfilling and peaceful outcomes.

- Review past situations when you were choosing between options (eg, should I do 'a' or 'b'). Rather than focusing on the choices, did you pray for the best outcome for everyone involved? Did you find this prayer 'choosing' the path to fulfill itself—the harmonious thought somehow accomplishing the prayer on its own? Practice choosing thoughts, words, and actions that are harmonious and non-harmful, and see if your life becomes embedded with these energies. The law of *karma* says, *as you sow so shall you reap*. So by thinking positive, harmonious thoughts, such peace returns to you manifold. When you make a choice, imagine the best of all possible future outcomes in your mind, and see if this vision comes to pass.

- Consider the most notable times in your life that were particularly pleasant or difficult. Try to remember how the event began. Did challenging beginnings yield wonderful results? Did an overly pleasurable start result in long-term trouble? Correlate these experiences with Lord Krishna's teaching, 'what starts as poison ends in pleasure, and what starts as pleasure ends in poison'. Does it help you make better decisions resulting in greater peace in life?

- Review the qualities of a Self-Realized person on page 181. Which qualities would you most like to exhibit in your life? Sincerely pray for these qualities to grow and consciously make choices to think, speak, and act in those ways. When you are making a decision, ask yourself which choice would a person with this divine quality make and follow through with it. Can you feel yourself come to life? Do you feel your self-esteem rise?

- Finally, review all the exercises in this book. If you have kept a journal, review your feelings and insights, and see how much you have changed since you began these exercises. Taking stock of your spiritual growth, and observing real growth, inspires a person to take bigger spiritual steps, set greater spiritual goals, and listen to higher spiritual visions. Return to your journal or these exercises every 6 months to a year, like spring spiritual cleaning, to monitor your progress towards your goals in your personal, family, and career life. You likely will discover more meaning in your life and ever-growing peace and harmony.

May God bless you with peace and harmony.

Aum Shanti Shanti Shanti

*Krishna's ancient wisdom is universal,
and can lead one peacefully through these modern times*

About the Author

Swami Sadashiva Tirtha received sannyas in 1991 from his guruji, Swami Narayan Tirtha, in his guruji's ashram, Shankar Math, in Uttarkashi (Himalayas). Since then, Swamiji has visited his guruji yearly until his mahasamadhi (demise) in 2001.

Swamiji is a part of the dual Siddhayoga Tirtha lineage. Tirtha is a lineage created by Adi Shankaracharya (788—820 CE), and is more recently known through Shankaracharya Bharati Krishna Tirtha, who, at the invitation of Paramhamsa Yogananda, was the first Shankaracharya to visit the USA. The Siddhayoga lineage is traced from Swamiji's guru, Swami Narayan Tirtha to his guru, Swami Shankar Purushottam Tirtha, to Narayan Dev Tirtha and to his teacher Swami Gangadhar Tirth Maharaj.

He founded the Swami Narayan Tirtha Math in his guruji's name (swaminarayantirtha.org), and published two books by his Param Guruji (grandfather guruji—Swami Shankar Purushottam Tirtha); *Yoga Vani, Instructions for the Attainment of Siddhayoga*, and *Guru Bani, 100 Ways to Attain Inner Peace*.

Swamiji has written two books, *The Ayurveda Encyclopedia*, and the *Ayurveda Primer* (e-book), and is a published Ayurvedic researcher.

He is certified in Ayurveda, Vastu Shastra, and Jyotish, and earned a Doctor of Science in Ayurvedic Research.

Swamiji spends his time in the ashram and does some writing, guiding people to realize peace in their daily lives.

surfer balanced,
wave does the work,
surfer enjoys the ride.

person balanced,
life does the work
person enjoys the ride.

- Swami Sadashiva Tirtha

Resources

Other books by Swami SadashivaTirtha

Ayurveda Encyclopedia: Natural Secrets to Healing, Prevention, & Longevity. Now in its 2nd edition—more than 20,000 books in print and an *amazon.com* top 10 Ayurveda-category best-seller since its publication in 1998. This book covers all aspects of the subject, spiritual, life-purpose, lifestyle, emotional/physical health and balance; scientific research, more. Therapies include herbs, nutrition, aromas, yoga, and meditation. [686 pages -8.25 x 11"]

This is also available as an e-book at ebooks.com)

Ayurveda Primer: Introduction, Case Studies, & Research (e-book). Clear, concise introduction to the subject. Questions most frequently asked by beginners are covered. Also included, simple guided meditation exercises and audio pronunciations of words. (download available at *vedicvendor.com*)

Spiritual Books from Sat Yuga Press

by Swami Shankar Purushottam Tirtha.

The author was requested to substitute as the Shankaracharya while H.H. Bharati Krishna Tirtha came to the USA at the invitation of Paramhamsa Yogananda. Thereafter he elected to leave the seat and return to his secluded ashram.

Yoga Vani: Instructions for the Attainment of Siddhayoga. This book discusses the authentic spiritual life—originally published decades before Western influence. Written in an easy-to-read, teacher-student question and answer conversation, the topics addressed include the meaning of *Siddhayoga*, gunas; experiences of asanas, pranayama, mudras; diksha (spiritual initiation), true Gurus, mantras, nada, kundalini shakti, deities, hatha, laya, raja yogas; yama-niyama, how to meditate, experiences in sadhana (meditation), the three bodies, more. 194 pgs.

Guru Bani: 100 Ways to Know Peace. This book addresses how to live a spiritual life outside of meditation. Short essays extracted from talks given by Swamiji to his disciples—some married, others monks. Pure teachings from an ancient time untouched by modernism. 59 pgs.

Both books available at at http://vedicvendor.com

Swami Sadashiva Tirtha's Web Sites

1. Swami Narayan Tirtha Math

This site discusses the spiritual philosophy and history of the author's guru, Swami Narayan Tirtha. Specifically it talks about his dual Siddhayoga and Tirtha lineages. Also available are spiritual articles, poems, pictures, and letters by this great saint. See full details at http://swaminarayantirtha.org

2. Ayurveda Holistic Community

This site is a free educational online community. It offers Ayurveda article and research journals where hundreds of articles by Ayurvedic doctors from India and around the world freely share their expertise. http://ayurvedahc.com/

The online Research Ayurveda Journal publishes abstracts on research and case studies. http://www.ayurvedahc.com/articlelive/categories/Research-Ayurveda-Journal/

Shakti Ayurveda Magazine (available only as an online e-zine) covers Ayurveda, Spirituality, Ecological, Renewable energy, Alternative Education, Social/Fair Trade ideas, poetry, book reviews, and more. Free sign up at: http://ayurvedahc.com/

Suggested translations of Bhagavad Gita

Books
Srimad Bhagavad Gita
By Swami Paramananda
Vedanta Centre Publishers
Cohasset, MA, USA

The Bhagavad Gita:
According to Gandhi
Berkley Hills Books
Berkley, California, USA

Online:
http://www.bhagavad-gita.org/Gita/verse-02-01.html
http://www.asitis.com/6/20-23.html
http://webapps.uni-koeln.de/tamil/

Reader Feedback

Do you have questions, comments, or a story how this book has helped transform your thinking and life experiences? Do you have a parallel between ideas from your religion and those discussed in the

Gita? Log onto our website (http://*satyuga.com*) and send Swamiji your feedback. We will post online reader comments and questions that will benefit others as well, and may use comments to update future editions of the book.

Sat Yuga Press books

Find information about our mission and all our books; reader comments and suggestions—what to add in future editions, ideas for new books, and author information. http://*satyuga.com*

Sat Yuga Press is an 'socio-eco-positive' publisher - using recycled papers, organic and non-toxic products; offsetting carbon emissions, tree and water usage in both our professional and personal lives and donating more for resources than we use. In this way we stop harming mother nature and rejuvenate her as well.

Our recycled paper usage exceeds the Green Press Initiative's 5-year goals for responsible publishers [greenpressinitiative.org]. Our paper supplier is a zero-carbon company, and our printer is also an environmentally conscious company.

We also support free-trade and other uniquely successful social programs that help people around the world to help themselves improve their economic, educational, and health situations.

See our socio-eco-positive policy online at satyuga.com

Lord, thank you for the best day possible